Relatively Speaking

A Comedy by
ALAN AYCKBOURN

D1240845

Evans

Evans Plays   London

Printed in Great Britain by offset lithography by Billing & Sons Limited, Guildford and London

237 49483 3   PR. 1557

Reprinted 1970

INTRODUCTION

In general, the people who liked this play when it was first seen remarked that it was 'well constructed'; those that didn't called it old-fashioned. If the latter is true, then I suppose it's because, as the song goes, I am too. As to whether it's well constructed, well, in a way I hope it is, since I did set out consciously to write a 'well made' play. I think this is important for a playwright to do at least once in his life, since as in any science, he cannot begin to shatter theatrical convention or break golden rules until he is reasonably sure in himself what they are and how they were arrived at.

And this knowledge is really only acquired as a result of having plays produced, torn apart and reassembled by actors and held up to public scrutiny for praise or ridicule. I suppose I am extremely lucky, writing for a small theatre company as I did for so many years, to have had almost a dozen plays put through this very process before reaching the age of thirty. Not only this, but to have had to fight all the limitations of a small theatre – the number of actors available, difficulties of staging, even lighting complications – and, most important, being aware that if my play didn't at least break even at the box office, we'd all be out of a job on Monday. I wrote, in a sense, to order, and there was no harm in this, since the order was always of a technical nature and dealt only minimally with content. But there is no sharper lesson for a dramatist than to find himself sharing a dressing-room with an actor for whom he has written an impossible quick change.

I wrote this play originally as a result of a phone call from the late Stephen Joseph, a truly remarkable man of the theatre, without whose unrelenting deadlines this would never have been written and to whom I dedicate the play, sadly, but with great affection. He asked me then simply for a play which would make people laugh when their seaside summer holidays were spoiled by the rain and they came into the theatre to get dry before trudging back to their landladies. This seemed to me as worthwhile a reason for writing a play as any, so I tried to comply. I hope I have succeeded.

ALAN AYCKBOURN

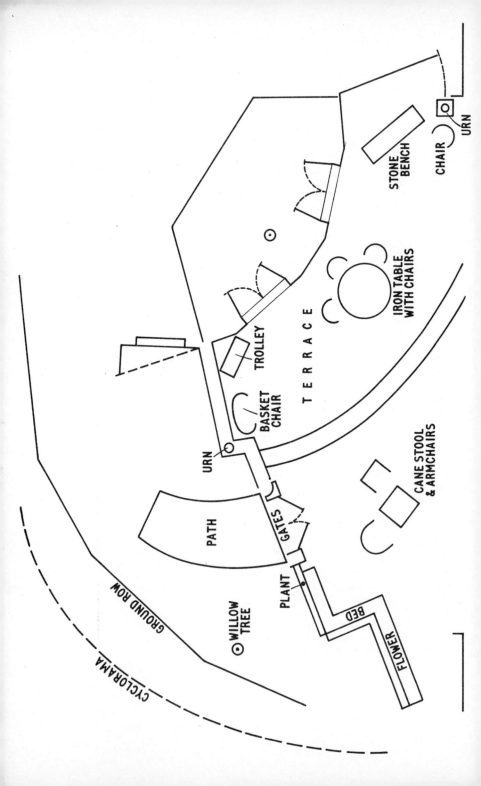

RELATIVELY SPEAKING

This play was presented by Peter Bridge at the Duke of York's Theatre, London, on 29th March 1967, with the following cast:

GREG	Richard Briers
GINNY	Jennifer Hilary
PHILIP	Michael Hordern
SHEILA	Celia Johnson

Directed by NIGEL PATRICK

Designed by HUTCHINSON SCOTT

The action of this play takes place during a summer weekend in London and the country.

No character in this play is intended to portray any specific person alive or dead.

RELATIVELY SPEAKING

ACT I

Scene 1

London, Sunday 7 a.m.
A bed sitting room furnished by someone young,
slightly zany and very feminine. A few posters on
the walls, a doll or so, female bric a brac.

Two doors lead off - one to the bathroom, the other
is the front door of the apartment. A series of
elaborate screens in one corner of the room conceals
the kitchen area. Other furnishings include an easy
chair, a couple of upright chairs, a folding table, a
chest of drawers and a single divan bed.

The curtains are drawn back a fraction allowing a
shaft of morning light into the otherwise darkened
room.

At the start GREG is in bed, though only discernible
as a mountain of bedclothes.

The phone rings. Again. And again. Running water
sounds from the bathroom but no one answers.

Then an arm snakes out from under the bedclothes,
gropes for the phone and eventually draws the
receiver back with it under the bedclothes.

GREG   (muffled)   Hallo. 3467. Hallo. Hallo.
          (Emerging from bedclothes.)   Hallo. Who is that?
          Hall-

(The caller has evidently rung off sharply. GREG
eyes the telephone suspiciously. Replaces the
receiver. Sits up properly. Looks around him.
Blinks. He starts to get out of bed but realising he is
naked he wraps the loose top sheet around himself. It
makes a rather elaborate loin cloth. GREG rises and
crossing to the window, draws the curtains. More
splashings from the bathroom. GREG moves over this
way. He catches sight of himself in the mirror.)

(Gravely.)   The return of Sabu. Anybody seen an
elephant?

(The phone rings again. GREG frowns, turns and
moves to the phone. Thinks. Lifts the receiver.)

(In disguised Indian voice.)   Hallo, this is 3467, can
I help you please.   (Pause. Normal voice.)
Hallo. 3467. Who is that? Hall-   (He hangs up
slowly. After a moment's thought he moves
determinedly towards the bathroom.)   Ginny! Ginny!
(Treading on something sharp.)   Ginny - aaaah!
(He hops about.)

GINNY   (off)   What?

(GREG returns to the bed, sits, and twists his foot
to examine the injured sole of his foot.)

(Off.)   Greg?   (Sticking a tousled head round the
door.)   Greg - Oh. Did you call?

GREG   No.

GINNY   What are you doing?

GREG   Just reading my fortune.

GINNY   Was that the phone?

GREG   When?

GINNY   Just now?

GREG   (slight pause)   No.

GINNY   Oh. You sure?

GREG   (still studying his foot)   According to this I'm going
to meet much trial and tribulation but will eventually
find true love and marry a girl with a birthmark on
her left thigh. Nobody I know.

GINNY   Nor me.

GREG   I'll keep a look out.

GINNY   It's not a birthmark. It's a beauty spot.   (Disappears into the bathroom again.)   Kettle should be boiling. I put it on.

GREG   Good.   (He is staring at the phone again.)

GINNY   Make the tea, darling, or I'll never be ready. The alarm didn't go off. As usual.

            (As he talks GREG is absently fishing under the bed with his feet.)

GREG   Don't usually need one in this bed. It's so narrow one of us falls out automatically as a rule. We ought to market it.   (His feet have now found a pair of smart black men's slippers. He rises and crosses U.R. to the kitchen area. The slippers are evidently far too large for him. They make loud slapping noises on the floor as he walks. He disappears behind the screens.) What time's your train then?

GINNY   (off)   Eight twenty-four.

GREG   (out of sight - in a loaded tone)   Oh well. Have a good time, won't you?

GINNY   (after a slight pause appears in the doorway)   Greg.

GREG   (head round the screens)   Yes?

GINNY   Stop it.   (She goes back into the bathroom.)

GREG   (grimaces and disappears too)   Oh hell, no.

GINNY   What?

GREG   (out of sight)   More of them.

GINNY   (anxious head around door)   What?

GREG   (appearing with a bunch of flowers)   Bloody flowers. All over the place. In the sink here as well.

GINNY   (offhand)   Oh, those.

GREG   Where are you working these days, for heaven's sake, Kew Gardens?

GINNY   I like them.

GREG   So do I - in their place. But they're moulting all over everything in here.

GINNY   (extending a naked arm)   Give them to me. I'll put them in the bath.

GREG   (to her)   Fine.   Plant some water lilies while you're
           there.

GINNY   Have you made the tea?

GREG   Just about.   (Returns behind the screen for a
           second.)

           (GINNY disappears back into the bathroom.)

           Aaagh! Petals in the kettle.   (He emerges from
           behind the screen with two mugs and a teapot. He
           places these on the table D.C.)

GINNY   (appearing at the bathroom door — she is clad in her
           underclothes and is pulling on a dressing gown)
           Hallo, lovely.   (She moves to him below coffee table
           D.C.)

GREG   Wotcher gorgeous.   (He kisses her lightly.)

GINNY   Will you miss me today?

GREG   (slight pause)   Mmmmm?

GINNY   I said will you miss me today?

GREG   Miss you? Me? No, I'll be having a great time.
           Action packed, simply thrilling day. Parties, parties
           all the way, what?   (A merry military laugh.)

GINNY   I'll miss you too.

GREG   (nodding but seemingly unconvinced)   Mmmmm.
           (He turns and plods back U.R. towards the kitchen
           area.)

           (GINNY glances after him, gives a shrug and
           disappears once again into the bathroom. GREG
           stops in his tracks abruptly. Stands for a second as
           if listening for something, stares at his feet and
           then proceeds on his way.)

GINNY   (off)   My God. Look at the time. I'll never make it.

           (GREG returns, this time with the sugar basin and a
           half-filled bottle of milk. He stops again and stares
           hard and long at his feet.)

           (Re-enters, brushing her hair.)   I must have some
           tea, I'm —   (Taking in GREG.)   What's wrong?

GREG   Nothing. I got the idea someone was following me, that's all.   (He crosses to above coffee table and puts down milk and sugar.)

GINNY   My God! My husband - !

GREG   Could be -

GINNY   (with a dramatic look at the front door, moving C. to GREG as she speaks)   Oswald. How did you find out?

GREG   (clutching GINNY to him)   No, sir - I insist. Shoot us both if you're going to shoot -

GINNY   I love him, Oswald, I love him!

GREG   (backing U.L. with her)   We'll die together, I tell you. Go on, shoot - shoot, damn you! BANG!

(They both collapse on the bed in a mock death scene and giggle. GREG kisses her. They lie in each other's arms for a second.)

GINNY   (semi-apologetic)   I'm going to miss my train.

GREG   Who cares?

GINNY   (sitting up and breaking from him slightly)   No. I can't. (She rises, moves down to coffee table and sits R. of it. She pours the tea.)

(GREG after a second reaches for the cigarettes. He lights one and then, holding the packet in his hands, studies it intently. A pause.)

GREG   (turning his attention to her)   Let me guess what you're thinking about.

GINNY   (passing him tea)   You'll have a job. Here.

GREG   (moving down to L. of table)   Ta. I'll bet you were admiring my slippers.

GINNY   Your slippers?

GREG   (sitting L. of table, displaying his feet)   Look.

GINNY   What a daft idea.

GREG   Oh. You weren't?

GINNY   Sorry. No.

GREG   Oh.

GINNY   I didn't even know you'd got any.

GREG   Ah. That's just the point.

GINNY   What?

GREG   That is just the point.

GINNY   (looking at him, amused)   Honestly.

GREG   (toasting her in tea)   Cheers.

GINNY   I'll miss you.

GREG   Will you?

GINNY   Did you think I wouldn't, Greg?

GREG   Depends on how much you live it up, I suppose.

GINNY   With my parents? Don't make me laugh.

GREG   Then why go?

GINNY   It's only one day. I'll be back tonight.

GREG   One day? It's half a weekend.

GINNY   I haven't seen them for ages.

GREG   Ah. Duty.

GINNY   Partly. I'm fond of them too.

GREG   Would I like them?

GINNY   Yes - I think so.

GREG   Good. Can I come?

GINNY   Yes, you must.

GREG   Now. With you.

GINNY   For the hundredth time. I've told you they're not
            expecting you. I can't just bring someone down out
            of the blue. They'd never forgive me.

            (Pause. GREG rises and moves L. to bathroom.
            Turns. Looks at her.)

GREG   I'm very taken with these slippers, I must say. What
            do you think of them?

GINNY   What?

GREG   These. Did you like them?

GINNY   They're all right. Why?

GREG   I just wondered what you thought of them. That's all.

GINNY   Well – they're just – slippers, aren't they?

GREG   Yes. That about sums them up.   (Sits on bed. Pause.)

GINNY   (getting a little fed up now)   Am I supposed to have done something?

(GREG shrugs.)

Greg?

GREG   I don't know. Have you?

GINNY   I don't know. You're the one that's carrying on.

GREG   Me? I'm just quietly sitting here, that's all.

GINNY   Doing your best to annoy me.

GREG   Nonsense.

GINNY   Oh yes, you are.

GREG   (taunting)   Now why should I want to annoy you? Tell me, why should I want to do that?

GINNY   Oh go to hell.   (She rises and crosses to recess D.R. to fetch her dress; then turning.)   I think your bedroom slippers are simply bloody marvellous.

GREG   Thanks.

(GINNY goes and returns with her dress. GREG rises and marches towards the bathroom. He has abandoned his slippers by the bed. GINNY looks at him and laughs.)

(Turning.)   Mmmm?

GINNY   What do you look like?

GREG   What's wrong?

GINNY   Talk about me having birthmarks. You've got one.

GREG   Where?

GINNY   (pointing to his bottom)   There.

GREG   That's not a birthmark. That's a scar. This bottom has seen active service, I'll have you know.   (He goes into the bathroom.)

(GINNY smiles and starts dressing, U.C.)

(Off)   Oh for crying out loud! What _is_ going on?

GINNY   What?

GREG   (off)   This bath is full of flowers.

GINNY   (stops dressing)   Yes, I put them there. I said I was
          going to.

GREG   (off)   You put one bunch in the bath. That makes five
          altogether.

GINNY   (innocently)   Does it really?

          (GREG appears in the doorway festooned with dripping
          flowers.)

GREG   Five.   (He counts the other three bunches already
          displayed there.)   Five – six – seven – eight –
          Where do they come from?

GINNY   Those are the ones you brought me.

GREG   Mine are the two shilling bunch, I know.   Whose are
          these? Mmmm?

GINNY   Well, you know that little man who sells flowers on
          the cor er of the road – the one who has the stall?

GREG   No.

GINNY   Well, there's a little man at the corner of this road
          that sells flowers on a flower stall and he was selling
          them off cheaply – yesterday evening – Friday – end
          of the week. I thought I'd buy a bunch for the weekend
          and he said I could have five bunches for the price of
          two. I couldn't refuse, could I?

GREG   No.

GINNY   They were probably stolen.

GREG   From the Queen Mother's garden.

GINNY   (lamely)   Yes.

GREG   As long as I know.   (Turns as if to go back in,
          then to her again.)   Oh, by the way. Where did
          the other two come from?

GINNY   Oh, he gave me those as a present.

GREG   I see.   (He returns to the bathroom.)

          (During the next section GINNY finishes dressing
          and starts to make up in the mirror. GREG wanders
          in and out of the bathroom, dressing as he does so.)

GINNY   (calling)   Want some more tea?

GREG   (off)   Please.   Tell me.   What makes your parents
         so frightened of meeting strangers?

GINNY   They're not.   It's just that they're old-fashioned, I
         suppose.   They like to do things properly.

GREG   (emerging)   Don't you think they'll approve of me?

         (GINNY pours two cups of tea and milk and sugars
         them.)

GINNY   Of course they will.   My father's, well – he's a bit
         difficult, I suppose.   You know, he wants the best for
         me, at least what he thinks is the best for me.

GREG   I am the best.

GINNY   I know that.   But I've got to convince them, haven't I?
         And anyway, my mother gets into an awful panic if
         people arrive when she's unprepared.

         (GINNY moves up to mirror below bed and starts to
         make up.   She takes her tea with her, leaving GREG's
         on the table for him.   GREG comes out of the bathroom.
         He now has on his trousers and carries his socks and
         shirt and tie.)

         There's your tea.

GREG   Thanks.   (Moves to table, sits and puts on his
         socks.)

GINNY   What's the time?

GREG   Twenty to.

GINNY   (screaming)   I'm going to miss it.

GREG   Take a taxi.

GINNY   (making up frenziedly)   I knew it.

GREG   I'll phone for one.

GINNY   Damn – damn – damn.

GREG   I said I'll phone for a taxi.

GINNY   You'll have to.

         (GREG continues to put on his socks.)

         Well go on!

GREG   When I've got my socks on.

GINNY   Oh. You're no use at all.

GREG   (casually)   Who lives at the Willows, Lower Pendon,
           Bucks. ?

GINNY   (scatters her makeup – recovering)   How did you
           know that?

GREG   Who lives there?

GINNY   (moving down L. beside him)   Where did you find
           that address?

GREG   Sounds very grand. The Willows, Lower Pendon –

GINNY   Have you been going through my things?

GREG   No.

GINNY   Then tell me where you got that address from. I want
           to know.

GREG   It's written on here.   (Holding up cigarette packet.)
           Look. The Willows, Lower Pendon, Bucks. Anyone
           we know?

GINNY   (moving away to mirror again)   No.

GREG   (rising)   Who?

GINNY   (turning)   My parents.

GREG   (moving U.L.)   Ah. Well, you may have a lousy
           memory for all I know. I mean I could never be called
           a devoted son, my parents will back me up on that, but
           at least I can remember where they live.

GINNY   (flaring up defensively)   I wrote it down for someone
           at the office – a girl, but she forgot to take it. She
           knows them because we went to school together. She
           wanted to write to them. All right?

GREG   I believe you.

GINNY   Quite sure?

GREG   Yes.

GINNY   Quite?

GREG   Yes. Shut up.

           (GINNY takes a swig of tea.)

GINNY   You make tea like liquorice as well. I don't know why
           I put up with you.   (She moves past him towards the
           kitchen area.)

GREG   (penitently)   Tell me something.

GINNY   What?

GREG   Why <u>do</u> you put up with me?

GINNY   Well.

GREG   Well?

GINNY   Maybe for the same reason you put up with me. (Smiling, gently.)   You're a fantastic lover, if that's any consolation to you.   (She goes into the kitchen area.)

GREG   (to himself)   That's nice.   (He picks up the slippers, regards them. Sits R. of table.)

              (GINNY returns, having diluted her tea. She moves below him to sit L. of table. Just as she is about to sit GREG drops the slippers on to her chair.)

GINNY   Now, if we order a taxi in about five minutes, that should get me to the station with about ten minutes to spare. Don't forget I've got to buy my – aaaah. (She sits on the slippers. Reacts by jumping straight up again, spilling her tea in the saucer and slopping some on to the table.)   Oh, God!   (Seeing slippers.)   Oh, big joke.   (Throwing slippers on the floor.)   Hell, what a damn stupid thing to do. What's got into you?

GREG   (penitent again)   Sorry.   (He has risen too.)

GINNY   I should think so. Look at this. I'll have to get a cloth.   (She moves U.R. to kitchen, then turns back.)   Listen, if you're sick of me say so.

              (GREG sits unhappily R. of table, his back to her.)

              Well, we can't go on like this. It's daft. Isn't it?

GREG   (muttering)   If that's how you feel –

GINNY   How I feel! That's marvellous. Look, I don't know what it is, but I hope you'll have got over it by tonight, that's all. I've got quite enough to worry about without being messed around by you.

GREG   (wheeling sharply)   And what the hell do you think you're doing to me?

GINNY   (taken aback)   What?

              (The phone rings. GINNY continues to look at GREG for a moment. Then she answers the phone, crossing above him.)

GINNY   Hello...yes...no, no...I'm afraid you have the wrong
         number...yes...Goodbye.   (She rings off.)

         (GREG has risen and moves D.R. to the alcove.)

         What did you mean just now?

GREG   (collecting and returning with a battered zipper bag)
         I'd better pack up.

GINNY   Greg - ?

GREG   Work it out during your jolly weekend at the Willows,
         Lower Pendon - (He crosses below table C. and into
         the bathroom.)

GINNY   Greg?

GREG   (off, sullen)   Get lost.   (He returns cramming some
         of his belongings into his zipper bag, his shaving kit
         etc. and a dirty shirt he has collected from the bathroom.
         He dumps his bag on the chair R. and finishes packing it.)

GINNY   Don't forget your beloved slippers, will you?

GREG   Oh, those.

GINNY   (picking them up and holding them out for him)   Here.

GREG   I don't want them, they're no use to me.

GINNY   Oh for heaven's sake! Take them.

GREG   What size are they, as a matter of interest?

GINNY   How should I know?

GREG   (sits and starts to put on his shoes, which he has
         retrieved from under the chair R.)   It'll be written
         on them somewhere, have a look. On the instep.

GINNY   Tens it says. Why?

GREG   No good to me. I take eights. See if they fit you.

GINNY   That's rather stupid, isn't it?

GREG   What is?

GINNY   Getting tens. I mean if you take eights -

GREG   I didn't get them.

GINNY   Who did?

GREG   No idea. My slippers are eights.

GINNY   Well, whose are these?

GREG   I don't know. I just found them lying about.   (He
         finishes tying his shoes.)

GINNY   Where?

GREG   Under your bed.   (Pause. GREG watches her.)

    (GINNY sits, slowly, on the bed.)

    Our bed. Or somebody's bed, anyway. That one, there. Perhaps it belongs to the bloke who owns the slippers.

GINNY   So that's it.

GREG   (rising and wandering right D.R. and then slowly up towards her)   It was rather odd really. When I got up just now I was a bit dozy, you know, and I did what I do at home – I fished with my feet under the bed for my slippers. One of my habits, that is, one of my idiosyncrasies – it helps me to recognise myself when I'm half asleep. I always think that's important, don't you? That the first thing you do when you wake up in the morning is to make sure you know who you are. I have a terror of that, losing my identity in the night. Some people are frightened of burglars breaking in. With me, it's stealthy midnight brainwashers. (Sitting beside her on the bed.)   Anyway, I did this fishing with my feet business, and I thought to myself, steady lad, you're in for a shock. They won't be there. This is her flat you're in. Don't panic now. You're the same person you were when you went to sleep. Only the bed has been changed. And then, the blow. A pair of alien slippers attached themselves to my toes. I can tell you that was an experience I wouldn't care to go through again. It could have split my personality right up the middle. Did you know that? Very nasty.

GINNY   You really do jump to conclusions, don't you?

GREG   In those slippers I do.

GINNY   (rising and up to the window)   You really do jump to conclusions.

GREG   Now and again. Like wondering why, when you pick up the phone, you say yes to someone and then no. I can't quite work that out.

GINNY   How do you mean?

GREG   Just now.   (He rises and moves down L.)   What did the person calling say when you answered the phone?

GINNY   I can't remember.

GREG   Whatever they said, you said yes. Did they say, is that 34_57_?

GINNY   (breaking D.R. away from him)   They might have done. Something like that. What's it matter?

GREG   No, they couldn't have done. Or you'd have said, no this is 34_67_.

GINNY   Where is this getting us? I'm in a hurry.   (Starts to move as if to her makeup.)

GREG   (stopping her)   Wait, this is interesting. On the other hand, did they say, is that 2467 and you thought they said 3467. Is that it?

GINNY   (sits on chair R. of table)   Maybe. I misheard them probably.

GREG   (moving in to L. of chair L.)   So they thought they'd got the right number?

GINNY   Yes - no, they didn't.

GREG   They must have done because you said yes. I mean, if I ring someone up and when they answer I say is that 2467 and they say yes, I'm rather inclined to take their word for it, aren't you?

GINNY   He soon realised his mistake anyway.

GREG   It was a him, was it? What did he say?

GINNY   (tiredly)   I don't know. He said, is that Jack or something.

             (Pause.)

GREG   I see. Jack. You said yes, and he said is that Jack? (Moving away D.L.)   Poor old Jack. There's something definitely wrong with Jack. Whatever happened to Jack, I wonder?

GINNY   Maybe he said Betty, I don't know. He said is that somebody-or-other and I said no.

GREG   Yes. Let's settle for Betty.

GINNY   Anything so long as you're happy.

GREG   (to her)   I should think Jack would be a lot happier too. I wonder who it could have been. Perhaps it was that funny little bloke who has a flower stall on the corner. He sounds as if he's a bit confused, poor old soul.

GINNY   All right? Satisfied? Happy? All settled? Good.

GREG	Thank you. I'll get you a taxi, shall I?
GINNY	Oh, thank <u>you</u>.

(GREG moves up to the bedside table and picks up the phone. Gets the number from the pad and dials.)

You don't trust me at all, do you?

GREG	(mock cheerfully) I shouldn't let it worry you.
GINNY	Well, it does. Because you get unbearable.
GREG	It must just be me and my simple mind. (He rises and rescues some shoes from under the bed.) Oh, hallo...yes, could I have a taxi please? Straight away. 41 Redbury Square. Yes. My name is Miss Whittaker. That's right. I'll be outside waiting. I'm wearing a blue dress and a white coat. Bye. (He hangs up.)
GINNY	(moving to him by the table and putting her arms round him) You're mad, do you know that you're a complete lunatic?
GREG	Um.
GINNY	We must make a resolution, never, never to say goodbye when we've just had a row, no matter. ' We must make it up first.
GREG	Okay.
GINNY	You know, I was thinking – the first time I ever saw you, remember?
GREG	It was only a month ago. I'm not the one with the lousy memory. Malcolm's party.
GINNY	That's right. I saw you sitting there and I thought – him. I want to get to know him. He looks interesting. He looks different from the rest of this lot. And I looked at you and I smiled and you scowled back at me – ever so sweetly. And I thought he doesn't like me. I'll make him like me. So I chatted you up.
GREG	And I thought who the hell's this garrulous bird, twittering away here sixteen to the dozen?
GINNY	(releasing him) I wasn't as bad as that.
GREG	What? (Moving D.R. to his bag.) Inside ten minutes you were telling me all about your unhappy experiences. I didn't know whether to kiss you or give you half a crown.
GINNY	Oh, happy times. (Turning back to mirror and

scooping up her belongings into her handbag.) Is the taxi here yet?

GREG   You'll be lucky.   (He moves to the window.)

GINNY   (moving to the bathroom)   I'll have to do my nails on the train.

GREG   No taxi.

GINNY   (off)   Darling, could you see if I've got any polish remover in the top drawer? It's a small white bottle.

GREG   Okay.   (He attempts to open the top drawer. It seems to be jammed.)   It's stuck.

GINNY   (off)   Oh, it often does that. Pull it out from underneath.

GREG   Fiendish cut-price oriental furniture –   (He goes to open the second drawer down. He pulls too hard. The drawer and all its contents are scattered over the floor.)   Hell!

(GINNY comes in abruptly when she hears the noise. She is in the middle of doing her hair. She carries the brush. GREG stands surveying the contents of the drawer. About five or six expensive boxes of chocolates.)

GINNY   Clumsy! I –   (She pulls up short.)

GREG   Developed a sweet tooth?

GINNY   Oh, those –

GREG   Yes.   (He bends and starts to pick them up.)   Who sold you these, then?

GINNY   No one. They're samples. Free samples. I know a girl you see, who works in a chocolate place. And she gets them free. Only she's dieting. So she gives them to me.

GREG   I thought you were dieting?

GINNY   Yes, I am. Only not as much as her though.

GREG   (decidedly unconvinced)   I see.

GINNY   (sensing this)   Well – where else did you think they came from?

GREG   Lots of explanations spring to mind. The most charitable one would be to say that they were left over from my predecessor.

GINNY   Who?

GREG   You know. The man you've forgotten all about.
        Remember?

GINNY   Oh, that was years ago. No.   (Turns to the mirror
        to finish her hair.)

GREG   I see.   (Continuing to tidy up.)   You never say much
        about him, do you?

GINNY   I told you.

GREG   Not much.

GINNY   It's all forgotten. I've - forgotten what he looks like
        even.

GREG   Where's he gone then?

GINNY   Back to his wife, I expect. I don't know.

GREG   The older man. Must be nice to be with someone your
        own age, isn't it? You two couldn't have had much in
        common. Did he give you lectures on the Boer War?
        (Refits the drawer and closes it.)

GINNY   Don't get bitchy.

GREG   Well -

GINNY   (turning to him)   Greg - what would you have done,
        if you'd ever met him?

GREG   (meaning it)   I'd have hit him. Hard.

GINNY   I believe you would.

GREG   Well, I'm damn glad for your sake he walked out on you,
        that's all.

GINNY   He didn't walk out on me. I walked out on him.

GREG   (over-sympathetically)   Of course.

GINNY   (slightly riled)   I did.   (She moves D.R. to the
        alcove for her coat.)

GREG   (soothing)   Yes, I'm sure you did. I was just thinking
        though, how often have you met someone who's been walked
        out on? I mean, I must know dozens of people all of whom
        have at one time or another walked out on someone. But
        I've very rarely met any of the people that they've walked
        out on.   (Sitting on bed.)   Don't you think that's very
        odd? Where do all these poor jilted people go to, that's
        what I want to know? They can't all be floating in the
        rivers, they'd be clogged up by now. Bit like elephants

when they die or flies in winter time, don't you think?

GINNY   (who has reappeared carrying her coat, which she
places on chair R.)   I really wouldn't know.

GREG   Why did you walk out on him?

GINNY   (sitting on chair R.)   I had my reasons.

GREG   Oh?

GINNY   Look, I'm not going to tell you so you may as well shut
up.

GREG   All right.   (He shrugs.)   All right.

GINNY   I don't see why you should be so interested, anyway.
I don't give a damn about your past life.

GREG   (smiling angelically)   Ah - but my life didn't begin
until I met you.

GINNY   (sarcastic)   Oh, yes.   (Springing up and moving to
window.)   Where the hell is that taxi?

GREG   He'll ring the bell when he gets here.

GINNY   Not if he's looking for a man in a blue dress and a
white coat he won't.   (To him and ruffling his hair,
then moving as if to cross him.)   Lunatic man.

GREG   (grasping both her hands)   Mmm. You know?
(Rising.)   I've been thinking - it might be a good idea
if we got married - pretty soon.

GINNY   When - now?

GREG   No.

GINNY   Oh, good. Going to say, I'd have to go and change my
dress again.

GREG   No. Seriously.

GINNY   When did you suddenly get this idea?

GREG   I thought it might be a good thing.

GINNY   (releasing his hands and stepping back, looking at him)
I take it you're proposing to me?

GREG   (up to window, uncertainly)   Yes, I suppose I am
really. If you look at it that way.

GINNY   Either you are or you aren't.

GREG   (turning)   Yes, I am.

GINNY   I see. I'm just going out - actually.

GREG   The taxi won't be here for a second. It doesn't take you that long to make up your mind, does it?

GINNY I'm afraid it does. (Pause. She sits on bed.) If you're serious, I don't know what to say. I love you very much, more than I've ever loved anybody, I think. And I think I'll probably say yes, one day. But not at the moment.

GREG I see.

GINNY Greg, have you really thought about this? I'm sorry to ask you - but you're not asking me away for a dirty weekend or something. Or even a dirty month.

GREG A dirty great life time. I know.

GINNY Who have you known apart from me? How many other girls?

GREG Well -

GINNY I mean really known - you know what I mean.

GREG Well - I - well -

GINNY I'm the first, aren't I?

GREG (injured) If it's that obvious -

GINNY It doesn't make any difference to me. But what about you? For all you know, compared with someone else I might be the biggest bitch on earth.

GREG You're not. (Slightly anxious.) Are you?

GINNY Be bad luck if we married and then you found out, wouldn't it?

GREG (R. to front door) What do you want me to do? Chase round? Knock on doors? Take a census?

GINNY I just want you to be sure, that's all.

GREG I am sure.

GINNY All right.

GREG I know what I'm doing, don't worry.

GINNY Fine. Good. (Rises and picks up her handbag from the table.)

  (Slight pause.)

GREG (down to chair R.) There's no chance that you'll have made up your mind in a couple of minutes, is there?

GINNY Why?

GREG   Well, I thought if I could come down with you now and
          see your parents, I could ask –

GINNY   No Greg!

GREG   It's only that –

GINNY   No.

GREG   But –

GINNY   No, no, no.

          (GREG looks downcast. GINNY moves to him at the
          table.)

          (Soothingly, kissing him lightly.)   Darling – darling
          – I can't –

          (Door bell rings.)

          Hell, there's the taxi. I'll have to run.   (Breaking
          from him and gathering up her things.)   Do you want
          to come and see me off?

          (GREG doesn't reply but mooches up to the window.)

          I'll be back about seven. You can come round and let
          yourself in if you like.

          (Door bell rings again.)

          (Muttering.)   I'm coming.

GREG   I don't want to worry you, but that's not the taxi
          driver.

GINNY   It isn't?

GREG   Not unless he's come round without his vehicle.
          There's no cab out here.

GINNY   Oh.   (Crossing quickly to the door.)   I'll see who
          it is.

GREG   (intercepting her)   I'll go.

GINNY   No, it's all right – let me –

GREG   I'll go.   (He has his hand on the door handle barring
          her way.)

GINNY   No.

GREG   (pushing her back gently but firmly with one hand and
          opening the door)   Won't be a second.

GINNY   (panicky)   But Greg!

          (Door bell rings.)

GREG   Wait there.

(He goes out, leaving the door ajar. GINNY stands uncertainly, crosses to the window, looks out nervously, back to the door and peers out. The phone rings. She jumps. GINNY peers out through the door again. Seeing GREG is occupied she hurries to the phone, picks it up and speaks in a low voice.)

GINNY   Yes... it is... now listen, I've had about as much as I can stand from you... oh, yes you do... we <u>have</u> discussed it... over and over again... no...

(GREG enters quietly. He stops and listens for a moment. Then withdraws.)

And if you ring me up again... because it's damned annoying to start with... yes... yes... yes. (She rings off.)

(Just as she is doing this, GREG enters gaily.)

GREG   Back again.

GINNY   Ah.

GREG   Surprise, surprise. It was a ginger lady. From next door. Parcel for you. She took it in.   (He holds it out.)   Look.

GINNY   Oh, yes.   (Pause.)   That's nice.   (Taking it.) Thank you.   (She stands holding it uselessly.)

GREG   Aren't you going to open it?

GINNY   No. Not now. It's only some stupid book. They keep sending them. I don't know why. I've asked them not to.

GREG   Who?

GINNY   These book people. I don't want it.   (She crams it into the waste paper basket.)   No use to me.

GREG   Oh.   (Pause.)   Was that the phone?

GINNY   When?

GREG   Just now?

GINNY   No. Must have been upstairs.

GREG   Oh, yes. That must have been it.   (He moves to the window and stands with his back to her, looking out.)

GINNY   (pacing about)   I'm wondering whether to start walking it, you know.   (Pause.)   I mean it'll only take me about ten minutes, won't it?   (Pause.)   Only if I sit round waiting for this taxi any longer, I'll miss the train.

I could walk it in ten minutes - couldn't I?

(GREG ignores her completely.)

(Suddenly.)   Oh. Do you know? I've just remembered. Where those slippers came from.

GREG   (turning)   Where?

GINNY   Did you ever meet Jane?

GREG   Jane who?

GINNY   The girl I used to share this flat with. No, you didn't. She left just before I met you.

GREG   (moving to examine slippers which are below table C.) Don't tell me they're hers?

GINNY   No. But she had a puppy.

GREG   A puppy?

GINNY   Well, a dog really. They were his.

GREG   Oh, I see.   (Pause.)   What was he, a Great Dane?

GINNY   No, he was a -

GREG   A St. Bernard.

GINNY   No, one of those little dogs.   Mmmmm -

GREG   Well, I'll say this for him. He may have only had two legs, poor little thing, but he had a fine big pair of feet for a dog of his age.

GINNY   A dachshund. That's it.

GREG   (moving to the bed and falling on his knees beside it) Hang on.

GINNY   What are you doing?

GREG   (reaching about under the bed)   Seeing if I can find the other pair. I can't bear this. The thought of that poor little puppy with two huge feet - staggering round this flat - hang on, wait a minute.   (Rising and back down L.) Perhaps he only wore those on his front legs. Perhaps he wore Wellington boots on his back legs for when he went out. Yes, that's it. He just changed feet, depending on whether he was coming in or going out. Clever dog.

GINNY   Have you finished?

GREG   Just about.

GINNY   Greg.

GREG   Mmmm?

GINNY   Trust me – please.

GREG   Yes?

            (Door bell rings.)

GINNY   I promise you.   There's no one else now, I promise.

GREG   Your taxi.

GINNY   There's no one else. Only you.

GREG   Nobody?

GINNY   No, no, no.

            (Distant door knocking.)

GREG   You'd better go.

GINNY   Yes.   (She gathers her things and moves to the door.)
            I love you.

GREG   (smiles and nods slowly)   Me you. Bye.

GINNY   See you.   (Kisses him.)

            She goes. After a moment the front door opens and
            slams distantly. GREG makes as if to depart too. As
            he passes the waste paper basket he stops. Overcome
            with curiosity he lifts out the parcel she has left there.
            Stares at it, feels it and then shakes it. It rattles.
            He tears a tiny hole in the wrapping and peers in.
            Frowns. Tears a larger hole. Stands still. Finally
            he rips the covering off altogether. From the midst of
            the brown paper and corrugated cardboard he pulls out
            a highly decorated, very expensive heart-shaped box of
            chocolates. A pause. GREG comes to a decision. He
            looks at his watch, grabs up his things, runs for the
            door. Stops, runs back for the cigarette packet, picks
            it up, glances at it briefly and then rushes from the
            room slamming the door behind him.

            CURTAIN

Scene 2

            Sunshine. A garden patio leading off from a large
            fairly modern house, in the Home Counties. This in
            turn leads off to the garden. PHILIP and SHEILA sit
            at breakfast, reading the Sunday papers. The birds
            sing.

PHILIP   I can't say I'm very taken with this marmalade.

SHEILA   No, nor am I.

PHILIP   Then why did you buy it?

SHEILA   I couldn't tell by looking at it, could I?

PHILIP   Hm.   (He returns to his paper.)

SHEILA   They didn't have our sort.

PHILIP   I'd sooner have none than this.

SHEILA   You say that now. You say that –

PHILIP   If you ask me we'd have been a lot better off with jam.

SHEILA   You may well say that –

PHILIP   I do. I mean it.

          (A silence.)

SHEILA   More tea?

PHILIP   Yes – if there's a – if there's a ... yes.

SHEILA   (pours him a cup of tea)   There you are.

          (PHILIP grunts.)

          Are you playing golf this morning?

PHILIP   I don't think so.

SHEILA   It's a beautiful day.

PHILIP   Yes.

SHEILA   Be lovely for you up there. Up there on a day like this.

PHILIP   Up where?

SHEILA   (gesticulating vaguely)   Up there. On the rinks.

PHILIP   The rinks?

SHEILA   Oh, darling... The golf rinks.

PHILIP   Links.

SHEILA   Mmm?

PHILIP   Links. Golf links or cuff links. Ice rinks.

SHEILA   Work you up an appetite. I'd go if I were you.

PHILIP   I think you can safely allow me to arrange my own morning.

SHEILA   All right. I thought it would invigorate you, that's all.

PHILIP   Don't be late for church, will you?

SHEILA   I'm not going this morning.

PHILIP   No?

SHEILA   It's the third Sunday after Epiphany. I never do.

PHILIP   Ah.   (He looks baffled.)

SHEILA   That man from Dodworth comes over to preach. And we
         all know about him.

PHILIP   Oh, I see.   (PHILIP reads his paper. He laughs
         suddenly.)   Very amusing piece here. It says... er..
         'Eighty-four per cent of the people questioned said
         that...' Oh... Oh, I see.

SHEILA   Said what?

PHILIP   Nothing. Nothing.

SHEILA   Said what?

PHILIP   Nothing. I thought it was amusing but it isn't .

SHEILA   Oh.

         (Silence.)

PHILIP   No letter this morning?

SHEILA   I'm afraid not.

PHILIP   No? None at all?

SHEILA   Not really.

PHILIP   Oh dear. Someone's slipping.

SHEILA   What do you mean by that?

PHILIP   I don't really expect letters today so I'm not disappointed.
         But you must be.

SHEILA   I don't know what you mean.

PHILIP   I mean, of the two people living in this house you're the
         only one who ever gets a letter on a Sunday. I mean, on
         a Sunday - whoever heard of letters on a Sunday? I've
         never had any - never. I'm quite jealous.

SHEILA   It only happened once.

PHILIP   Once is enough, surely.

SHEILA   I've told you. It was a mistake -

PHILIP   So you said.

SHEILA   By the Post Office.

PHILIP   Ah!

(A pause.)

SHEILA   It's nice to have you home.

PHILIP   Mmmm.

SHEILA   I see so little of you these days.

PHILIP   Oh, I don't know.

SHEILA   You're always off somewhere.

PHILIP   Can't be home all the time. Don't want to overdo a good thing, do we?

SHEILA   Heavens no. Heavens no.

PHILIP   Well then. And you want time to yourself too.

SHEILA   What for?

PHILIP   Other things.

SHEILA   Oh, yes.

PHILIP   Look at the Coopers. Married nearly thirty years. Couldn't have a happier couple. I'm sure it's because he spends nine months of the year in Rio de Janeiro.

SHEILA   I hope you don't intend to follow suit?

PHILIP   Oh, no. I don't fancy South America at all.

SHEILA   What about this European business? The trip you were planning.

PHILIP   Oh, that. It's not really settled.

SHEILA   I hope it doesn't fall through. I was rather looking forward to that.

PHILIP   You're still keen on the idea then?

SHEILA   Of course. Aren't you?

PHILIP   I've been making a few enquiries about it. What exactly it entails. Really rather dull.

SHEILA   Dull?

PHILIP   Not going to be much of a holiday. More of a race. France, Germany, Italy, Spain, Switzerland, Holland, Denmark and Sweden. All over in ten days. Travelling overnight. Chasing from railway station to railway station. Very tiring and not much fun.

SHEILA   Didn't sound like that when you mentioned it the other day.

PHILIP   That's what it is.

SHEILA   So you'd rather I didn't come?

PHILIP   It's entirely up to you. I can't see you enjoying it for a moment.

SHEILA   No?

PHILIP   Suit yourself, though.

SHEILA   All right. I'll stay behind.

PHILIP   Probably have a better time if you do. Get me out of the way for a couple of weeks.

SHEILA   Ten days.

PHILIP   More or less.

           (Pause.)

SHEILA   Won't you be lonely on your own?

PHILIP   I must say it's odd your getting letters at weekends.

SHEILA   Why?

PHILIP   Well, I mean. Here I am away most of the week and here you are getting letters on Saturdays and Sundays. Not the way I'd carry on.

SHEILA   We seem to have had this conversation before.

PHILIP   Surely half the fun of having an affair is keeping it a secret.

SHEILA   Maybe for you.

PHILIP   I'm speaking theoretically. But now the game's up – I've found out.   (Pause.)   What joint have you got today?

SHEILA   Pork.

PHILIP   Very nice. With lots of crackling, I hope?

SHEILA   Oh, yes – swimming in it.

PHILIP   Hardly the phrase I'd use. Think I'll have a go at the garden today. Well, make a start anyway. Get stuck into those vegetables. Have you seen it lately – the kitchen garden!

SHEILA   No.

PHILIP   Absolutely fantastic. Couple of weeks, that's all, and you ought to see it – absolutely knee deep in them. Weeds, nettles, thistles. The lot. And those creeping

things – whajermacallits? Look like French beans lying
down. Of course, knowing that garden, they might well
be. Don't think so though, they look far too healthy.
Have to be careful, though, hacked my way straight
through the rhubarb last time. Do you remember that?
All that ruddy rhubarb? Even had it for tea. This
book's no help either, never seems to mention anything
I grow. I can't recognise them from the illustrations
anyway. Still, I suppose all nature looks different in
black and white. I think we ought to get a man in, you
know. Be better off in the long run, someone from the
village – someone who really knows. Your chap doesn't
know anything about gardens, does he?

SHEILA   No.

PHILIP   Pity. Might have worked out quite well if he had.

SHEILA   Well, he doesn't. (SHEILA hesitates as she is about to
depart.)   I might go down to Kent for a weekend,
before long.

PHILIP   Sorry?

SHEILA   I might go down to Kent for the weekend, soon.

PHILIP   Why?

SHEILA   I'd like the change. Natalie's written and asked me.

PHILIP   Natalie?

SHEILA   She's my cousin.

PHILIP   Your cousin?

SHEILA   That's right. She's got a cottage there and she's
invited me for a long weekend.

PHILIP   I didn't know you had a cousin called Natalie.

SHEILA   No, I don't mention her much. She's getting on.

PHILIP   Oh well. Go ahead.

SHEILA   You don't mind?

PHILIP   Not in the least.

SHEILA   (flatly)   Good. That's settled then.   (She turns to go.)

PHILIP   Sheila ...

SHEILA   Yes?

PHILIP   (coaxing)   Come on ....

SHEILA   What?

PHILIP   Oh, let's stop all this, shall we? You know, I know,
         we both know. What's the point?

SHEILA   Point?

PHILIP   Why keep on with it? What are you trying to prove?

SHEILA   I'm afraid I don't quite follow you.

PHILIP   (getting angry)   Oh, for the love of Mike, woman,
         what do you think you're achieving by all this nonsense?
         Eh? You're not fooling anyone by it, you know. You're
         certainly not fooling me and what's more you know you're
         not. So why bother to keep on with it?

SHEILA   What?

PHILIP   You know what, well enough. This fatuous rigmarole.
         Every damn weekend. I feel I'm humouring a lunatic
         half the time. Is he coming today? Has he written?
         Has he phoned? Well, I've played along long enough.
         I'm sick and tired of it, do you hear? That's it. I
         seriously think you ought to go and see a doctor. You're
         ...   (Gesture of insanity.)

SHEILA   (after a pause)   Have you quite finished?

PHILIP   Yes.

SHEILA   I've never seen or heard such extraordinary behaviour
         in my life. Really. Whatever's come over you? I
         really think you ought to go and do some digging. And
         work a little of it off. Whatever it is.

PHILIP   No. I'll do some hoeing. I don't feel in the least like
         digging this morning.

SHEILA   From the way you do it, I can't see there's much
         difference - I'll go and get dressed.

         (PHILIP goes off up the garden. GREG enters the
         garden cautiously from the direction of the house. He
         hesitates when he sees SHEILA. He carries his bag
         and has a raincoat over his arm.)

GREG   (after a tentative pause)   Hallo.

SHEILA   (startled)   Oh. Oh - hallo there.

GREG   Hallo.

SHEILA   Are you - er...?

GREG   I beg your pardon?

SHEILA   Were you wanting to see someone?

GREG   Yes.

SHEILA   My husband?

GREG   Not ... altogether...

SHEILA   Me?

GRE G   Partly.

SHEILA   Oh, well then.

GREG   I did ring.

SHEILA   It doesn't work.   (She smiles.)   Won't you come in :

GREG   Thanks.   (He comes D.S.)

         (SHEILA remains standing.)

SHEILA   Do sit down.

GREG   Thanks. What a beautiful garden.   (Sits in armchair.)

SHEILA   Yes, we're ... fond of it ...

GREG   I had no idea it was going to be so nice. Beautiful.

SHEILA   Yes, it is nice, isn't it?

GREG   Look at those dirty great delphiniums. They're huge.
         How do you get your delphiniums that size?

SHEILA   Oh, well ... constant practice, really. My husband's
         green fingers.

GREG   They're like hollyhocks.   (Looking out over audience.)

SHEILA   Are you sure you mean delphiniums?

GREG   Well, those things. Whatever they are.

SHEILA   Oh, they're lupins.

GREG   Pretty good going, all the same.

SHEILA   Thank you.   (Pause.   She smiles a little uncertainly.)

GREG   This is the Willows, isn't it?

SHEILA   Yes.

GREG   Lower Pendon?

SHEILA   Oh, yes.

GREG   Bucks?

SHEILA   Yes, this is the Willows.

GREG   Oh, good. I suddenly had the sneaking feeling I'd got
          the wrong house.

SHEILA   The Willows.

GREG   That's the one.

          (Pause.)

SHEILA   You like our trees then?

GREG   Yes, I've just been admiring them.

SHEILA   There's something so majestic about trees, isn't there?

GREG   Regal.

SHEILA   Such a sense of – permanency.

GREG   Yes. You wouldn't shift that lot in a hurry.

SHEILA   Quite.   (Pause.)   We haven't met before have we?

GREG   Not to my knowledge.

SHEILA   No.

GREG   Seems almost as though we have, doesn't it?

SHEILA   (laughing)   Yes, yes, it does indeed.

          (Pause.)

GREG   Look, I know who you are. I'm Gregory.

SHEILA   Oh yes?

GREG   Greg.

SHEILA   Oh, Sheila. How do you do?

GREG   How do you do?

SHEILA   Have you come far?

GREG   From London.

SHEILA   By car?

GREG   No, train. I caught the early one. Specially...

SHEILA   Specially.   (Sudden thought.)   You didn't stop by
          for a glass of water, did you?

GREG   No. Why?

SHEILA   It just crossed my mind. People do quite often.

GREG   Really. It's not a spa, is it?

SHEILA   Where?

GREG   Here.

SHEILA   Oh, no. I don't think so. It may have been, but it's
          certainly not now. Mind you, I'm quite hopeless at
          history.

GREG   Oh.

SHEILA   You haven't come all this way for nothing, have you?

GREG   Why?

SHEILA   To take the waters. You weren't under the impression
          you could take the waters here, were you?

GREG   No.

SHEILA   Oh.

          (Pause. GREG is rather uneasy, and so is she.)

GREG   I seem to have got here first.

SHEILA   First?

GREG   Yes.

SHEILA   Are there more of you?

GREG   No, just her. But you see, she doesn't know I'm coming.

SHEILA   No?

GREG   No. She'll probably kill me when she sees me here.

SHEILA   Oh.

GREG   Hope you don't mind my arriving out of the blue like
          this?

SHEILA   Not at all.

GREG   The point is, I caught the same train as her you see. At
          least, I thought I had. Only she didn't know I was on it.
          She thought I was still at – home – only I wasn't. I was
          on the train. Her train. Only when I got off it to
          surprise her she wasn't on it. She'd missed it. So I
          came on up.

SHEILA   Oh, I see.

GREG   And no Ginny.

SHEILA   Mmmmmm ?

GREG   No Ginny –

SHEILA   No, I'm afraid not. There's some sherry, if you'd like.

GREG   Not just at the moment, thanks.

SHEILA   Sure?

GREG   Thanks all the same.

           (Pause.)

SHEILA   This is the first really hot spell we've had, isn't it?

GREG   I suppose it is.   (He stares at her.)   Incredible.

SHEILA   I beg your pardon?

GREG   Quite incredible.   (He smiles at her and shakes his head.)

SHEILA   I'm afraid I'm ... not following you.

GREG   I hope you don't mind me saying that? It was meant as a compliment.

SHEILA   Not at all.

GREG   It's just that - you're going to slaughter me, you're really going to slaughter me when I say this - I thought of you as older.

SHEILA   Older?

GREG   Yes, much older. I know this is silly, but I thought of you as a sort of grey haired, little old lady.

SHEILA   (laughing in a strained sort of way)   I wonder where you got that idea from?

GREG   Well - you always tend to imagine that everyone else has one like your own, don't you?

SHEILA   One what?

GREG   Mother.

SHEILA   Oh - yes, yes. Sorry, I'm being terribly dim all of a sudden.

GREG   That's all right. It's probably me. I get nervous at meeting new people. Not just you. Everybody. Even bus conductors. You know, there's some mornings, I get on a bus and, I don't know if you feel the same, but I'm sitting there and there he is, the conductor, working his way down the bus towards me, and I think to myself, this morning I'm not going to be able to speak to this bloke. Not a word. He's going to say: Where to, mate? And I'm going to open my mouth and go huuuhhh... open my mouth and nothing comes out. So when I feel like this, I have to practise, you see. I sit there, saying it over to myself ... fourpenny one.... One morning I was doing this, I was rehearsing everything, even rehearsing the good morning I was going to say to my landlady... and I got on the bus and asked for ten cigarettes. I

                                  .

        couldn't speak for the rest of the day after that.

SHEILA (only slightly amused)   Yes, of course, I usually take the car.

GREG Ah well.

SHEILA Yes. The problem doesn't really arise. Though I do remember having to recite in front of the whole school once and feeling desperately nervous. I was very young of course. It was a competition, I think. For Memory and Elocution. My mind went a complete blank, I'm afraid. I had to read it.

GREG Oh, what bad luck.

SHEILA Yes. But as it happens I won the prize anyway, so it all ended happily. That was the only one I ever did win, you know, the Memory and Elocution.

GREG What was the prize?

SHEILA I've forgotten.

        (Pause.)

GREG I don't know where she's got to. She ought to be here by now.

SHEILA Oh dear.

GREG Look, I may as well tell you now - you see, the point is - I asked Ginny last night you see.

SHEILA You did?

GREG We want to get married.

SHEILA Really?

GREG Yes.

SHEILA Congratulations.

GREG You're not upset?

SHEILA Me?

GREG Yes.

SHEILA Why should I be?

GREG You never know, do you?

SHEILA I suppose not.

GREG And you think that - knowing what you do about me, which isn't much admittedly - that it'll work out?

SHEILA   What?

GREG   Our getting married?

SHEILA   Yes, I should think so. You look healthy enough.   If
          you - love each other.

GREG   Oh, yes.

SHEILA   Then I don't see why not. Of course, I don't really know.

GREG   Enough. No, quite.   (He smiles reassuringly. Pause.)
          I knew we'd get on. I told her. She said you'd scream
          when you saw me.

SHEILA   Why's that?

GREG   Oh, she painted a fantastic picture of you. You don't
          know. She said that when an extra person turned up for
          lunch, you just went into a panic. That sort of thing.

SHEILA   She did?

GREG   Yes.

SHEILA   This is Ginny, is it?

GREG   Yes. She obviously doesn't know you, does she?

SHEILA   No. Not at all.

GREG   Perhaps she was trying to put me off. That's a
          possibility. Hadn't thought of that.

SHEILA   What?

GREG   Subliminal jealousy. You know.

SHEILA   Oh?

GREG   Comes of being weaned too early or something.

SHEILA   Oh.

GREG   They say that bottle feeding's never the same, don't
          they?

SHEILA   Do they?

GREG   That's what I read. No reflection on you, of course.

SHEILA   Quite. You said something about staying to lunch?

GREG   That's kind of you. Thank you.

SHEILA   You're very welcome. I think I must - make a start -
          if you'll excuse me. I can't think where my husband
          has got to -

GREG   Can I give you a hand?

SHEILA   Oh, I don't know that—

GREG   I've got plenty of time to talk to him, haven't I? And
          I'm marvellous with potatoes.

SHEILA   Oh well, thank you then. Since you're here, you're
          here. Come inside. I'll make us some coffee.

GREG   I can leave my bag here, can't I?

SHEILA   Bag? Yes, that'll be all right. Unless it rains.

GREG   You needn't worry. I'm not planning to stay for the
          week or anything. It's just that I don't feel secure
          unless I've got it. Never know where you might finish
          up, do you?

SHEILA   Very true.

GREG   I can grab a word with your husband when he's finished,
          can't I?

SHEILA   Yes I should. I'm sure he'll be of much more help to
          you than I've been. Now, I really must make a start on
          lunch.

GREG   Tell me, is he easy?

SHEILA   Easy?

GREG   I mean, he prefers it if you're absolutely plain with him
          does he?

SHEILA   Yes, he can't bear anything fancy.

GREG   Fine.

SHEILA   Good plain English food — that's Philip.

GREG   Eh?

SHEILA   The only thing he can't bear at any price is onions.

GREG   Onions?

SHEILA   Yes, it's odd isn't it? I adore them.

          (PHILIP enters. He has been gardening. His sleeves
          rolled up and a pair of gardening boots. He is hot and
          disgruntled. He stops as he sees GREG and SHEILA
          close in conversation. He stares.)

GREG   No, I didn't actually mean that.

SHEILA   You didn't?

GREG   No — I was talking about me and her.

SHEILA   You and her?

GREG   Yes.

(PHILIP clears his throat.)

SHEILA   Oh – did you want something, dear?

PHILIP   I can't find the hoe.

SHEILA   How annoying.

PHILIP   (staring at GREG)   Yes.

SHEILA   Oh, Philip, this is Gregory. This is my husband, Philip.

GREG   How do you do?   (He rises and they shake hands.)

PHILIP   How do you do?

GREG   Just been admiring your garden.

PHILIP   Oh, yes?

GREG   You seem to have put a lot of work into it.

PHILIP   Yes.

GREG   Still, it's paid off. Very impressive.

PHILIP   Glad you think so.

GREG   No onions, I notice, eh?   (He laughs.)

PHILIP   You've met my wife, have you?

SHEILA   Of course.

GREG   Yes, thank you. We've been having a long chat.

PHILIP   Good.

SHEILA   Perhaps you two would like to have a word now?

GREG   Well –

PHILIP   What about?

SHEILA   I believe Gregory wants to ask you something.

PHILIP   Does he?

SHEILA   I believe so.

PHILIP   What?

SHEILA   I think you ought to ask him that. I'd better go.

PHILIP   Why?

SHEILA   Well, it's a personal matter really, I think.

PHILIP   Is it?

GREG   Sort of.

PHILIP   Oh. We haven't met before, have we?

GREG   No.

PHILIP   Hmm. Would you take a seat Mr. – ?

GREG   Poynter.   (He sits.)

SHEILA   I'll bring out the coffee in a moment.

PHILIP   Just a minute. Just a minute.   (Draws her aside.)
          Who is he?

SHEILA   I should ask him. He came to see you.

PHILIP   I've never seen him before. What does he want?

SHEILA   Something personal. You heard what he said.

PHILIP   What?

SHEILA   Ask him.   (To them both.)   I'll just slip away then.

          (SHEILA goes in. A silence. PHILIP moves about
          uncertainly giving GREG an occasional side-long glance.
          GREG rises as if to speak.)

PHILIP   Do sit down, Mr. –

GREG   (sitting)   Thanks.

PHILIP   My wife tells me you want a word with me.

GREG   That's right.

PHILIP   Ah.

GREG   Been hard at it have you?

PHILIP   Eh?

GREG   The garden.

PHILIP   Ah. Yes. Constant battle.

GREG   Man against nature.

PHILIP   Quite.

GREG   I'd offer to give you a hand, only I'd probably uproot
          all your flowers.

PHILIP   That'd never do. Can't have two of us doing that.

          (They laugh. Pause.)

          Was it – er – anything important?

GREG   Yes, as a matter of fact.

PHILIP   Ah.   (Pause.)   Come far?

GREG   From London.

PHILIP   Really?

          (Pause.)

GREG   It's a bit awkward in a way –

PHILIP   Oh?

GREG   I seem to have plunged in the deep end. I mean, it was
          only this morning that I woke up and suddenly decided
          that I'd come and see you – and now – here I am.

PHILIP   I see.

GREG   Yes.

PHILIP   Yes. It's not a bad train service.

GREG   I don't really know how much you know, that's the point.

PHILIP   Nothing.

GREG   Oh.

PHILIP   I'm afraid I've even forgotten your name.

GREG   Gregory.

PHILIP   Ah.

GREG   She said nothing then?

PHILIP   About what?

GREG   To you – about us?

PHILIP   You and me?

GREG   No, me and her.

PHILIP   You and her?

GREG   Yes.

          (Pause. PHILIP is puzzled.)

PHILIP   You and her?   (Dawning.)   You mean – her and you?

GREG   Us.

          (Pause. PHILIP looks at him.)

PHILIP   (slowly)   I see.

GREG   She has?

PHILIP   Oh, yes indeed she has. Oh yes, yes. She's told me
          about you. She's told me. You needn't worry about that.

GREG.   Oh. Good. It makes it that bit easier.

PHILIP   Makes what easier?

GREG   What I came to ask you.

PHILIP   Oh yes, she's told me. And the letters.

GREG   Letters?

PHILIP   Oh yes. And you thought you'd drop in and see me today, did you?

GREG   Yes.

PHILIP   How kind. I hope you weren't expecting something violent to happen on my part? I don't intend to engage in a free fight. Nor shall I go upstairs and shoot myself. Two popularly recommended courses, I believe.

GREG   You do know why I'm here, don't you?

PHILIP   I think you can safely leave me to work that out for myself.

GREG   You don't have to.

PHILIP   I'd rather.

GREG   Oh.   (Pause.)   You know, I was in two minds whether or not to come this morning. I thought, have I got the courage to ask him?

PHILIP   You're managing very well.

GREG   Thanks.

PHILIP   I can almost imagine you might have done it before?

GREG   Oh, no. Not on your life. The point is, you see, she doesn't know I'm asking you this.

PHILIP   She doesn't.

GREG   No. But then I thought, what have I got to lose?

PHILIP   Very little, I imagine.

GREG   Exactly. I thought, good grief, he won't eat me. So here I am. If you want to ask me any questions, go ahead.

PHILIP   Yes. What are your immediate plans then?

GREG   Ah, well.

PHILIP   You don't mind my asking?

GREG   No. Well – we're easy, you know. Don't want to rush things. Mind you, I'm not one for long engage- ments. So if it fits in with your plans I thought we'd get married sometime after Christmas.

PHILIP   Married?

GREG   Yes.

PHILIP   (after a pause)   You're not without a sense of humour,
           Mr. - ?

GREG   No.   Luckily.   I believe that it can come in very handy
           in a marriage.

PHILIP   Indeed it can.   Indeed it can.

GREG   I am at present earning sixteen pounds a week less
           insurance, in an insurance company and I'm told I have
           excellent prospects of promotion after fifteen years.
           Before that I was, amongst other things, a shoe salesman,
           an under-gardener for the G.L.C. - I got sacked from
           that.   A part-time postman and a temporary porter at
           Euston Station.

PHILIP   Sixteen pounds, hmm?

GREG   That's right.

PHILIP   Oh well, you should be able to buy her a good breakfast
           anyhow.   That's the important thing.

GREG   (smiling)   I'll do my best to throw in the occasional
           lunch as well.   How about that?

PHILIP   I doubt it.   Not on sixteen pounds a week less insurance.

GREG   I don't know.

PHILIP   I do.   I've kept her.

GREG   Other people manage.

PHILIP   Ah, but they're not her, are they?   She's unique.

GREG   (lovingly)   Yes, she's certainly that.

PHILIP   I worked it out once.   She costs me thirty quid a week to
           run and that doesn't include over-heads.   You'd better
           speed up that promotion of yours, laddie.   Tackle your
           boss first thing tomorrow morning.   Tell him that owing
           to unforeseen circumstances your cost of living has
           trebled overnight.

GREG   I see.   (He broods.)   I take it you're not altogether
           satisfied with my financial position?   You don't think I
           can keep her in the manner to which she is accustomed -
           and all that?

PHILIP   Well, nobody could do that.   She tends to become accustomed to a little more each year.

GREG   I can't say I've noticed her overspending. I don't know
        how long it will be before I get a rise.

PHILIP How long have you been with the firm?

GREG   Three weeks.

PHILIP Yes. Might be a little premature to stick in a pay
        claim. It certainly poses a problem, doesn't it? Pity
        you're no gardener.

GREG   So I take it you're turning me down on purely financial
        grounds, is that it?

PHILIP I'm not. But I think she might.

GREG   She knows how much I earn. She's prepared to risk it.

PHILIP Is she?

GREG   Yes.   (A pause.)

PHILIP (suddenly)   All right. Carry on.

GREG   You mean you give your consent?

PHILIP I've very little option.

GREG   We can get married?

PHILIP No, I'm afraid that's quite out of the question.

GREG   Uh?

PHILIP I think I ought to get you straight on one or two things,
        young feller-me-lad. As far as I'm concerned you can
        leave whenever you like and go wherever you like. You
        have my blessings. My only conditions are these. I am
        not prepared to finance you and marriage is completely
        out of the question.

GREG   But - ?

PHILIP You must understand that a man in my position can't
        possibly afford that sort of publicity.

GREG   In other words you'd sooner we lived together than got
        married?

PHILIP Far sooner.

GREG   (studying him)   You're a bit round the twist, aren't
        you?

PHILIP Am I?

GREG   From where I'm sitting you are. What's all this about publicity?

PHILIP   Come now –

GREG   What's wrong with getting married? I've read some pretty funny things lately, but –

PHILIP   It's rather who you're marrying, don't you think?

GREG   Meaning I'm a dead let down. Is that it?

PHILIP   Not at all.

GREG   Oh, yes. I know what's at the back of that mind of yours.

PHILIP   I think, under the circumstances, I'm being extremely reasonable.

GREG   You think that, do you? Well, I want you to listen to me for a minute. I'm doing you a favour, did you know that ? No, I bet you didn't. Well, I'll tell you. First of all, I'm not the first one. Still, that's nothing out of the ordinary.

PHILIP   Isn't it?

GREG   Not these days mate, you're out of touch. But do you know who she was knocking about with before me?

PHILIP   Before?

GREG   Some bloke who's old enough to be her father – that's who.

PHILIP   What?

GREG   Yes. I thought that would shake you. Some randy old man about thirty years older than she is, who's got bored with his marriage and decided to muck up her life. It just so happens I love her enough not to want to see that happen.

PHILIP   Thirty years?

GREG   At least.

PHILIP   Remarkable old gentleman.

GREG   You don't believe me?

PHILIP   It does sound rather –

GREG   I've got proof.

PHILIP   Where?

GREG   In my bag.

PHILIP   What?

GREG   I'll show you.

PHILIP   Wait. Do you mean to tell me that there have been others?

GREG   So I gathered - she doesn't say much.

PHILIP   How many?

GREG   Well - the average number.

PHILIP   And what is the average number?

GREG   Well, I don't know - about four or five.

PHILIP   My God!   (Pause.)   Four or five?

GREG   At least.

PHILIP   Men?

GREG   Presumably.

PHILIP   I -

GREG   I should think it over.

          (PHILIP does.)

PHILIP   Well, well, well, Mr. -

GREG   Poynter.

PHILIP   One lives and learns. Yes, one certainly does.

          (SHEILA enters with tray of sherry glasses.)

SHEILA   Hope I've chosen a good moment.

GREG   Oh, hallo.

SHEILA   I thought we'd all have a sherry instead.

GREG   Thank you.

SHEILA   It really is glorious out here, isn't it?   (Passing glass to PHILIP.)   Sherry dear?   Greg?

GREG   Thank you. This is very kind.   (Takes glass.)

SHEILA   A pleasure. Well, cheers.   (Puts tray on table.)

GREG   Cheers.

          (They sit and drink. Silence.)

SHEILA   Have you boys been chatting then?

GREG   Yes, we - aired one or two topics.

SHEILA   All satisfactory, I hope. I didn't know whether you'd finished or not. I peeped out and it looked as though you had.

GREG   I hope we didn't keep you cooped up indoors?

SHEILA   No, I peeled some vegetables. That sort of thing. I thought we'd have a cosy little lunch out here, just the three of us.

(PHILIP snorts.)

Are you all right dear? It's not too sweet for you?

(PHILIP bangs down his glass.)

Philip!

PHILIP   (angrily, glaring at her)   I've mislaid the hoe. Do you know that?

SHEILA   Yes, dear. So you said.

PHILIP   I had a feeling it was you who used it last.

SHEILA   Oh, no dear.

(PHILIP begins to pace around the garden in increasingly agitated circles. They watch him.)

PHILIP   I hope you realise that my entire morning has been wasted I might just as well have sat here reading my paper, or had a round of golf like I wanted to in the first place. I'd have been far better off. As it is, I've spent my whole morning searching for something that should have been put back in its proper place to begin with.

SHEILA   I'm so sorry.

PHILIP   So you should be.

SHEILA   Why me?

PHILIP   You had it last.

SHEILA   I did not dear. You are quite mistaken.

PHILIP   (bellowing)   You had it last. I distinctly remember.

SHEILA   (shrilly)   No.

GREG   (lamely)   Perhaps it's in the shed.

(A silence. PHILIP stands impotently, beside himself with rage, looking from one to the other. He moves to the table. With a violent movement he sweeps the newspaper on to the ground.)

PHILIP   (fiercely)   Haven't I made that clear to you? I can't
          find it. It's gone, vanished – completely disappeared.
          (Picks up GREG's bag from stool.)

SHEILA   What are you doing?

PHILIP   (pauses for breath; shouting)   Looking for the hoe!

SHEILA   (icily)   It won't be in there, will it?

PHILIP   Hardly likely, I should think.   (He strides off up the
          garden.)

          (SHEILA and GREG stand for a moment.)

SHEILA   What on earth was the matter with him?

GREG   No idea.

SHEILA   You didn't have an argument?

GREG   Not really. A sort of – animated discussion I suppose
          you'd call it.

SHEILA   Oh, yes. He's fond of those. Especially at breakfast
          or in cinemas. I don't think we've been to a film for
          years without having an animated discussion in the
          middle of it.

GREG   He's got – some fairly original ideas, hasn't he?

SHEILA   Has he?

GREG   Haven't you noticed?

SHEILA   I've probably got used to them, I've heard them so often.

GREG   His views on marriage.

SHEILA   Really?

GREG   He doesn't believe in it, apparently.

SHEILA   No. I have noticed from time to time. I think it's me he
          objects to really.

GREG   No, this is general. He doesn't believe in it for anyone.

SHEILA   That's a relief. I always took it rather personally.

GREG   On the other hand, I suppose he could just have disapproved
          of me.

SHEILA   Oh, I'm sure he didn't. Anyway, you don't want to take too
          much notice of what he says –

GREG   I was pretty blunt with him I suppose.

SHEILA   Would you like me to try and smooth things over for you?

GREG   That might help. Would you?

SHEILA   He'll probably get even angrier, but I'll try. Anything
          in particular you'd like me to say?

GREG   Well, it's just that I know so little about this sort of
          business.

SHEILA   Business? Oh, I see, well – are there any particular
          qualifications that you'd like brought out. I mean,
          obviously you don't want me to recommend you for
          shorthand and typing?

GREG   No. Hardly.

SHEILA   I think if I say that you display qualities of leadership,
          have a strong character and a modest, likeable
          disposition, with a good head for figures, that will
          cover a multitude of sins, won't it?

GREG   Do you think so?

SHEILA   You'd better pop into the house then. I'll come in and
          tell you how I've got on.

GREG   Right. Are you sure you know what you're doing?

SHEILA   I'll be as quick as I can. Providing I can find him.
          Straight through and on the left. Oh, and would you
          turn the oven down a point when you get there?

          (GREG goes in.)

SHEILA   (calling)   Philip! Philip!   (She moves off up the
          garden slightly.)

          (GINNY enters. She looks around, sees no one and
          with sudden purpose moves stealthily towards the house.
          SHEILA reappears and sees her.)

SHEILA   Oh –

GINNY   Oh –   (She stands, confused.)

SHEILA   Were you – ?

GINNY   This is the Willows, isn't it?

SHEILA   Yes. Lower Pendon.   (Pause.)   Bucks.

          CURTAIN

ACT II

Scene 1

The same scene. A moment later.

> A pause.

SHEILA You'll like our tree then?

GINNY Beautiful, yes.

SHEILA There's something so majestic about trees, isn't there?

GINNY Yes.

SHEILA Such a sense of permanency. I mean – you wouldn't shift that lot in a hurry, would you?

GINNY No, I suppose not.

> (Pause.)

SHEILA I was actually looking for my husband. You didn't see anybody just now, did you?

GINNY No.

SHEILA Perhaps he's hiding in the shed. He does that sometimes, when he's upset.

GINNY Why's he upset?

SHEILA I don't know. That's why I'm looking for him.

GINNY Oh.

SHEILA Did you want someone?

GINNY   I'm sorry - I'm Ginny Whittaker.   (Putting down her handbag.)

SHEILA   Sheila Carter. How do you do.   (They shake hands.)

GINNY   How do you do.

SHEILA   <u>Ginny</u>! <u>You're</u> Ginny?

GINNY   You've heard about me?

SHEILA   Oh, yes.

GINNY   He's told you?

SHEILA   Just now. All about you.

GINNY   I see. Well -

SHEILA   (taking GINNY's hand and leading her on to terrace) I'm so glad you've come. He was getting rather worried.

GINNY   Was he?

SHEILA   Yes, very.

GINNY   You don't seem very bothered?

             (They sit at table.)

SHEILA   You're just like I imagined you would be.

GINNY   Am I?

SHEILA   From what he told me. I hope you'll forgive my saying so but I think you'll make a lovely couple. Sherry?

GINNY   No, thank you.

SHEILA   I do hope everything works out for you.

GINNY   Works out?

SHEILA   When you're married.

GINNY   Married?

SHEILA   We were just this minute saying, no matter how much you think you know someone it's always a gamble in the end. Don't you agree? Oh, perhaps I shouldn't have said anything. I think he was going to explain everything to you himself. You are staying to lunch, aren't you?

GINNY   Well -

SHEILA   Good.   (Rises and moves to U.S. door.)

GINNY   Do you think I could possibly have a word with your husband?

SHEILA   My husband?

GINNY   Yes, it's a business matter –

SHEILA   (blankly)   Business?

GINNY   Yes.

SHEILA   Whittaker. You're Miss <u>Whittaker</u>? You work for my
         husband?

GINNY   I used to – surely you knew that?

SHEILA   Isn't that extraordinary! Of course I knew. How
         stupid of me. I'm so sorry. It was just that I got the
         impression from my husband that you were much older.

GINNY   Really?

SHEILA   Yes. I could have sworn he said you were due for
         retirement. That's why I didn't know your name was
         Ginny. Or anyway, that you were the same Ginny.
         He used to refer to you as 'Old Miss Whittaker.'
         (With a laugh.)   Perhaps he thought I'd be jealous.

GINNY   Perhaps he did.

SHEILA   He's very considerate. I'll see if I can rouse him.
         Maybe when he hears you're here – ?

GINNY   Yes. That should rouse him.

SHEILA   (calling)   Philip! Philip!

PHILIP   (distant)   What?

SHEILA   (calling)   Miss Whittaker's here to see you.

PHILIP   (distant)   Who?

SHEILA   (calling)   Miss Whittaker.

         (A far away crash of falling garden tools.)

         He's coming.

         (PHILIP enters U.S. of garden wall.)

         Look who's here.

PHILIP   Ah. Miss Whittaker!   (Leans on gatepost.)

SHEILA   We've met at last. I take it you two want to chåt. I'll
         go then. I can tell when I'm in the way.   (She smiles.)

GINNY   Thank you.

SHEILA   (confidentially to GINNY)   Hope everything works out
         all right.

         (SHEILA goes off through U.S. door on terrace. PHILIP
         watches her go, then looks at GINNY. He is silent for a
         moment. GINNY moves to below cane armchair and picks
         up her handbag.)

PHILIP   (moving towards her – sotto voce)   What are you
            doing here?

GINNY   I thought your wife went to church?   (Takes
            cigarettes and lighter out of her bag.)

PHILIP   Not on the third Sunday after Epiphany.

GINNY   Mmm?

PHILIP   Mr. Dodsworth –

GINNY   What?

PHILIP   Nothing.   She didn't.

GINNY   You've told her?

PHILIP   Told her what?

GINNY   About us?

PHILIP   I haven't told her anything.

GINNY   (putting her bag on stool)   Well, she knows.
            (Moving R.)   Hasn't she said anything to you?

PHILIP   Not a word.   (Moving D.L.)   Not about that. Not
            about us.

GINNY   She just told me that we make a lovely couple.   And
            she doesn't seem to care.

PHILIP   No.   Well, she has her mind on other things just at
            the moment.   What are you doing here?

GINNY   (sitting in cane armchair)   This alters things a lot.

PHILIP   What does?

GINNY   Her knowing.

PHILIP   Don't you mean – her going?

GINNY   Going?

PHILIP   Yes.   Somewhere in Kent.   (Moving to R. of GINNY.)

GINNY   She's leaving you?   How do you know?

PHILIP   She told me.   Or rather, he told me.

GINNY   Who?

PHILIP   The man in the kitchen.

GINNY   Who?

PHILIP   I don't know.   (Moves on to lower step of terrace at
            L.C.)   Some sallow youth.   Just now.   He came out
            here, stood there in front of me, calm as you like, and
            then asked me if they could get married.   Married – to

my wife!

GINNY He didn't?

PHILIP You're not losing a wife, you're gaining a brother-in-law. All that sort of thing.

GINNY What did you do?

PHILIP I was as co-operative as I could be. Refused the divorce of course.   (Moving to L. of GINNY.)

GINNY I bet you did.

PHILIP But told them they could go where they liked as far as I was concerned. After all, it's a heaven sent opportunity as far as we're concerned, isn't it?

GINNY We?

PHILIP Who else?

GINNY No, Philip.

PHILIP No?   (Bending over at L. of GINNY.)

GINNY (pause)   There's someone else.

PHILIP I know.

GINNY How?

PHILIP (moving L.C.)   I spoke to him on the phone last night.

GINNY You what?

PHILIP It's all right. No cause for alarm.

GINNY Damn you, Philip.   (Rises, backs to R. of armchair.) Damn you!

PHILIP Now don't get worked up. I rang off as soon as he answered.

GINNY No. Damn you. This is serious. This time I'm getting married.

PHILIP Are you?

GINNY He's asked me.

PHILIP (laughing)   Infectious, this marriage epidemic. seem to be the only one who's developed immunity. (Moves R.)

GINNY Philip, if you mess things up for me, I'll never forgive you.

PHILIP   (sitting in canvas chair)   Does he know about me?

GINNY   A little.

PHILIP   Is he jealous?

GINNY   He's human.

PHILIP   Does he know where you are today?

GINNY   Why?

PHILIP   He doesn't, does he?

GINNY   No. He thinks I'm visiting my parents, if you must know.

PHILIP   Your who?

GINNY   Well, I could be, couldn't I?

PHILIP   They're in Australia!   (Laughs.)   You really ask for trouble, don't you? One of these days – (Rises, moves on to lower step of terrace, U.S. of GINNY.)   I'd hate to lead a life as complicated as yours.

GINNY   He'll never know.

PHILIP   Unless someone tells him?

GINNY   They won't.

          (PHILIP moves to behind GINNY and puts his arms round her.)

PHILIP   You have been avoiding me, haven't you?

GINNY   (moving away)   Don't.

PHILIP   Why not?

GINNY   Your wife. They could easily see us through the window.

PHILIP   Don't worry. They'll be far too concerned wondering whether we're looking in at them.

GINNY   (now frosty and determined)   Philip – you must understand, this has got to stop. It's over. Leave me alone.

PHILIP   (injured)   I have.

GINNY   You have not. All those flowers, the chocolates, the phone calls – it's not fair on me, Philip. Can't you see that?   (Turns to face him.)   Please leave me alone.

PHILIP   Is that why you came all the way down here – to tell me that?

GINNY   Yes. That is it.

PHILIP   Right.   (Pause.)

GINNY   And I want those letters back.

PHILIP   Ah. That's more like it.

GINNY   (firm)   Please - Philip -

PHILIP   Think they might be safer where they are.

GINNY   Where are they?

PHILIP   Safe.

GINNY   Are you going to let me have them or not?

PHILIP   I don't know. They mean rather a lot to me, you see.
         Sentimental value and all that.

GINNY   (moving to him - appealing)   Philip, please.

PHILIP   You know, they've been very clever. Much cleverer
         than we have. I really think I've under-estimated that
         woman. Here we were, skulking in the shadows,
         meeting in obscure pubs, inventing elaborate alibis,
         telephoning secretly at two a. m. in the morning. While
         they, on the other hand - well, he's been writing to her
         quite openly. She even read his letters over the break-
         fast table.

GINNY   And you said nothing?

PHILIP   I didn't believe it. I didn't think any illicit romance
         could be conducted like that. In fact, I more than once
         accused her of making the whole thing up.

GINNY   Why should she?

PHILIP   To annoy me, I suppose.

GINNY   To make you jealous?   (Sitting at R. of table.)

PHILIP   I thought she'd - somehow got an idea I was carrying on
         with someone and had - invented this man -   (He
         laughs.)   I actually thought she was writing letters to
         herself. It was all rather pathetic. Rather amusing.
         Until the man turns up here in person.

GINNY   I see.

PHILIP   He's not the first either. There's been five others -

GINNY   Five?

PHILIP   Including a man of seventy, apparently. That really
         was a blow to my pride. Oh, well, her life's her own
         from now on.   (Sits in cane armchair.)

GINNY   You'll let her go?

PHILIP   She's going.

GINNY   (rising and turning U.S.)   Don't you think if you went in there now, this minute, and told her about us, everything, she'd change her mind?

PHILIP   I don't see why.

GINNY   Isn't that really all she's waiting for? For you to tell her the truth?

PHILIP   You may be right. But this is supposing that I do want her back, isn't it?

GINNY   Philip - be honest. Could you really do without her? (Kneels by PHILIP's chair.)   Ask yourself, as you're sitting there now, full of the breakfast that she's cooked for you, sitting in the sunshine, waiting for the lunch that's bound to be coming - and the tea and the supper. And you know she'll have made the bed for you, not like me. You'll even get your glass of hot milk, I expect. And your clean shirt in the morning, and your change of socks. They'll be waiting when you get up. And that's all Sheila. I bet she even cleans the bath out after you, doesn't she?

PHILIP   (muttering)   Now and again.

GINNY   Then make it up with her.   (Rising.)   Before it's too late.

PHILIP   (rising and moving to her)   I might.

GINNY   You must. Don't you see, Philip, you belong together - much more than we ever did.

(PHILIP nods and starts to move off - stands by gate-post.)

PHILIP   Tell you what, I'll think the matter over.

GINNY   Where are you going?

PHILIP   Look for the hoe. Want to come?

GINNY   Philip, I warn you. I'll - I'll go in there and tell her myself - everything.

PHILIP   If you can catch her attention, you're welcome.

(GINNY moves as if to go into house, but stops short of U.S. door.)

Go ahead, by all means, go ahead. Hoe!   (He goes off up the garden singing "Hi ho" etc.)

GINNY   (shouting after him)   Philip! All right, then, all right.

(GREG enters behind her, clad in an apron and bearing a tray, with tablecloth, knives, forks, spoons, four small plates, salt and pepper. GINNY turns, resolutely, as if to march straight into the house and comes face to face with him.)

GREG   Ah! At last.   (He kisses her cheek.)

(GINNY stands frozen. GREG puts tray on chair by table.)

I thought you'd got lost or something. I got here first.

GINNY   (weakly)   Greg –   (Moves to R. of table.)

GREG   Like my apron? Think it rather suits me. It's your mother's.   (He puts used sherry glasses on to tray on table.)

GINNY   Mother's?

GREG   We're having a busy morning.   (He picks up sherry tray and puts it on trolley, brushing past GINNY, who backs into U.S. door.)   So sorry.

GINNY   Who?

GREG   Me and your parents.

GINNY   What have you been saying?   (Gets between him and table.)

GREG   (brushes past GINNY again – picks up tablecloth) So sorry – all right, all right, don't look so worried. Nothing terrible. I haven't sworn all morning –

GINNY   What are you doing here?

GREG   (spreading cloth)   If you hadn't missed the train it would have been all right. I presume you missed the train?

GINNY   Greg, you idiot, I told you not to come.

(GREG goes round table, smoothing cloth. GINNY follows him.)

GREG   Why not? We're getting on like a house on fire. At least, your mother and I are.   (Lays side plates.) In fact, she's even putting in a good word for me with the old man. See if she can persuade him.

GINNY   To do what?

GREG   Let us get married, of course.

(GREG puts cutlery in bunch on table. GINNY sits on chair D.L. of bench. GREG moves towards her.)

You were right about him, by the way –

GINNY   I was?

GREG   I'll say you were.

GINNY   What did he – say?

GREG   Well, he's eccentric, isn't he? Couldn't really get through to him. It might have been me, I don't know. He didn't take to the idea much, anyway.   (Moves round table, pushing in chairs.)   Perhaps you could have a word with him, too. Try and sort him out.

GINNY   Yes, yes, I will.

GREG   Good.

GINNY   Providing you're out of the way while I talk to him.

GREG   Oh yes, sure.   (Picks up tray from chair.)

GINNY   (rising and moving to him)   Why don't you leave quietly now? Get the next train back and I'll try and see what I can do.

GREG   I can't do that.

GINNY   Why not?

GREG   I've been invited to lunch. Your mother insisted. She'd be very hurt.

GINNY   But surely, if I –

GREG   No, I couldn't do that. I'll have to stay. I'll just keep out of the way for a bit if you like.

GINNY   You must go.

GREG   I can't. Be reasonable about it. Anyway, I'd better get back to my kitchen. I'm involved in a large scale cooking operation, rolling out pastry for your mother. Very satisfying. No wonder cooks are fulfilled people. Are you coming?   (Starts to go off through D.S. door.)

GINNY   Greg.

GREG   (coming back)   What?

GINNY   There's something I have to tell you.

GREG   Go on.

GINNY   When I do, you'll probably walk out of here and never

	want to see me again. You're right, you see, Greg, not to trust me –
GREG	What are you talking about?
GINNY	I'm trying to be honest with you. I don't know where to begin.
GREG	Well? What haven't you told me? You mean about the bloke on the phone? Is that it?
GINNY	That's part of it. Oh, where do I start? To begin with, Sheila, that woman in the kitchen, isn't my mother.
GREG	Isn't – ?
GINNY	No. I'm not her daughter. I'm no relation of hers at all. On top of that, I – oh God –
GREG	(moving towards her) Hey, hey, hey – it's all right.
GINNY	(tearful) I haven't finished –
GREG	You don't need to, you don't need to, love, I understand.
GINNY	But Greg –
GREG	That's enough. Now come on, sit down. (Seats her in canvas chair.) Take it calmly. Don't get yourself worked up. You're so highly strung. (He gives her his handkerchief.) Here. Mop up.
GINNY	Thank you. (She blows her nose.)
GREG	There we are! Better?
GINNY	Yes.
GREG	You've let this get on top of you, haven't you?
GINNY	(weakly) Have I?
GREG	Is that why you didn't want me to meet them? Is that it? You've been going round nursing this so-called guilty secret, (Pulls cane armchair towards GINNY and sits.) because you've been frightened to tell me?
GINNY	Yes.
GREG	All right. So she's not your real mother. So what? Nobody knows, do they? Even if they do, nobody's going to condemn you for it. Certainly not me.
GINNY	But Greg –
GREG	Why should I? I love you for you, not who your parents are, or were.

GINNY   What are – ?

GREG   Now come on, snap out of it. This isn't the Victorian age, you know. I'm not going to run off because of that. You should have told me, straight out, instead of bottling it up. All you had to say was, 'Greg, I'm illegitimate,' and I'd have said, 'O.K., fine.' That's all.

GINNY   What?

GREG   Come on, say it. You've got to lick this thing.

GINNY   Say what?

GREG   Say 'I'm illegitimate' – come on –

GINNY   Now, Greg –

GREG   I'm illegitimate. Say it.

GINNY   Greg, I –

GREG   Come on. I'm illegitimate –

GINNY   I'm –

GREG   – illegitimate.

GINNY   Illegitimate.

GREG   Again.

GINNY   I'm illegitimate.

GREG   Good, again.

    (SHEILA enters from D.S. door with bowl of fruit and four napkins. She pauses in doorway.)

GINNY   I'm illegitimate.

GREG   There you are. Once more. Yell it out.

GINNY   I'M ILLEGITIMATE!

GREG   Well done.

SHEILA   Hallo.

GREG   (rising)   Oh, hallo.

SHEILA   Having a tiff?

GREG   No, no. A bit of therapy.

SHEILA   Oh, that's nice.   (Puts bowl of fruit on trolley.) Lovely weather for it.

GREG   Yes.

SHEILA   (putting napkins on table)   Are you going to finish the pastry?

GREG   Of course.   (Moving on to terrace.)   Get kneading
           again. Coming in, Ginny? We can find her something
           to do, can't we?

SHEILA   Yes, I'm sure we can.

GREG   Come on, love.

           (GINNY rises – starts to edge towards gate.)

GINNY   (weakly)   Yes.

SHEILA   You two carry on. I'll just lay the table.   (Starts
           setting cutlery.)

GREG   Right.   (Takes GINNY's arm – leads her to U.S.
           door.)   Come on, this way. You ought to know
           your way around by now.

           (GREG and GINNY go in. PHILIP enters from D.R.
           He stops when he sees SHEILA. He clears his
           throat and starts rolling down shirt sleeves.)

SHEILA   (without turning round)   Hallo, dear. Been busy?

PHILIP   Yes.

SHEILA   I expect you're hungry. Lunch won't be long.

PHILIP   Ah.   (Pause.)   Sheila – I think we ought to
           straighten out one or two things.

SHEILA   Ought we?

PHILIP   I think so.

SHEILA   What sort of things?

PHILIP   Well, I'd like to know your plans.

SHEILA   Plans?

PHILIP   Yes. Your immediate plans.

SHEILA   Oh. Well, they're nothing very spectacular. I'll
           finish laying the table. Then I'm going back into the
           kitchen to see how they're getting on with the pastry.

PHILIP   I meant slightly further ahead than that. I don't think
           there's any need to be facetious.

SHEILA   Well – lunch – that's about all I've got to –

PHILIP   (moving on to terrace)   Sheila, for heaven's sake.
           This is no time for avoiding issues. We've got to
           face things sooner or later –

SHEILA   Don't shout, dear, don't shout. They can hear you
           in the road. We've got to face what?

PHILIP   Your future. How do you intend to spend the rest of
            your life?

SHEILA   Why do you ask me that? Is it insurance or something?

PHILIP   (shouting)   Sheila! Please, please – talk to me.
            For once, woman, when I ask a question, <u>try</u>, try to
            give me the answer to the same question and not one
            you happen to have made up. I am not talking about
            <u>lunch</u>, I am not talking about <u>insurance.</u> I am talking
            about you and that lout in the kitchen.

SHEILA   Lout?

PHILIP   The young man, then, who calmly accosted me in my
            beautiful garden and asked me if he could marry my
            wife.

SHEILA   Your wife? You mean me?

PHILIP   Yes.

SHEILA   You mean Gregory?

PHILIP   Yes.

SHEILA   Gregory asked you if he could marry me?

PHILIP   Don't start pretending you didn't know.

            (Pause.)

SHEILA   Have you been to the pub this morning?

PHILIP   No. Why?

SHEILA   Sounds as if you've been in there since last night.
            What on earth has come over you? Talk about me
            being hare-brained –

PHILIP   You deny it?

SHEILA   He certainly never mentioned it to me. Really, dear,
            you've got hold of entirely the wrong end of the stick.
            I don't know how you managed it. Let me put your
            mind at ease and say that Gregory has certainly no
            intention of wanting to marry me.

PHILIP   He hasn't?

SHEILA   Of course not. Anyway, it's out of the question.
            He's already engaged. Poor boy, no wonder he was
            confused. What have you been saying to him?

PHILIP   You also deny the four or five others?

SHEILA   What?

PHILIP   And the man of seventy?

SHEILA   Who's he?

PHILIP   Your lover.

SHEILA   Of seventy? Thank you very much. I'm flattered.

PHILIP   I see. I see.   (Pulls out chair at R. of table and
          sits. Pause.)

SHEILA   You know, I really think you ought to wear your hat
          when you're gardening in the sun, don't you?

PHILIP   So it's all – untrue?

SHEILA   Yes, dear.

PHILIP   There's no one else?

SHEILA   Ah-ha! Wouldn't you like to know?

PHILIP   But it's not – Gregory?

SHEILA   No, dear. Now why don't you sit down and have a
          nice rest? You look very hot and flustered and you've
          obviously been overdoing it again. Is it that hoe
          that's upset you?

PHILIP   What hoe?

SHEILA   Never mind. I'll tell you what, we'll all have a jolly
          good look for it after lunch, how's that? Now just sit
          quietly. Don't move.

          (GREG enters from D.S. door with bottle of wine.)

          Oh, thank you, Gregory, that's so kind of you.
          (Takes bottle and puts it on trolley.)

GREG   I've finished the pastry. It's as flat as it will go.

SHEILA   (picking up sherry tray and moving to U.S. door)
          Oh, I'll see to it now. (To GREG.)   Don't upset
          my husband again if you can help it.   (Goes
          through U.S. door – reappears at D.S. door and
          hisses at GREG.)   I think he's a little over-tired.

GREG   Oh, right.

          (SHEILA goes indoors again.)

          (Rather nervously.)   Hallo.

PHILIP   Hallo.   (Pause.)   I was just chewing over our
          chat together earlier –

GREG   Oh, were you?

PHILIP   Yes. I think we might have been – I think there
          might have been a certain amount of misunderstanding.

GREG   Really? I hope so.

PHILIP   So do I.   (Rises.)   You see, for reasons I can't
really begin to justify, really a rather complicated
set of circumstances –   (Moving slowly off terrace.
– following on a rather peculiar conversation that I'd
just been holding, led me to understand, quite
erroneously, that you wanted to marry my wife.
That's the impression I got at the time, anyway –

(Pause.)

GREG   You thought I wanted to marry your wife?

PHILIP   Yes.   Silly misunderstanding.

(Pause.)

GREG   She's married, isn't she?

PHILIP   Yes, yes quite.   (Moving about restlessly.)
got that idea from somewhere.

GREG   Very odd.

PHILIP   Yes.   (Pointing at GREG.)   You don't, do you?

GREG   What?

PHILIP   Want to marry her?

GREG   No.

PHILIP   Ah, well.   That little obstacle's out of the way'.
Always best to know where one stands in these
matters.

GREG   Yes.   (Pause.)   If you don't mind me saying, it
seems a rather peculiar thing to think, doesn't it?

PHILIP   I suppose it does.

GREG   Mind you, you must have thought I was rather
peculiar too, come to that.

PHILIP   I'm afraid I did, rather.

GREG   (moving to PHILIP)   You know, I got the impression
that you did.   It's a horrible feeling that, isn't it?
Knowing that someone is looking at you and thinking,
this is a peculiar person, and not knowing why they'r
thinking it.   Like arriving at a party in a new suit
with the label still stitched on the seat of your
trousers.

PHILIP   Really?   That's – not happened to me.

GREG   You're lucky then.   I make a habit of things like
that.   Not that particularly.   I've only had one suit
and that was father's.   But you know what I mean?

PHILIP	Oh, yes, yes.
GREG	I'm sorry you thought that.
PHILIP	Forget it. (Moving on to terrace.)
GREG	Thanks.
PHILIP	There is - there is just one small point, though.
GREG	What?
PHILIP	If you didn't really want to marry my wife, who was it you did want to marry?
GREG	Well - your daughter.
PHILIP	Ah. (Pause.) My daughter. (Gropes for back of chair at U.S. of table.)
GREG	That's right.
PHILIP	You want to marry my daughter, do you?
GREG	If you don't mind?
PHILIP	Ah, well. Now you have posed a bit of a problem.
GREG	Have I?
PHILIP	It's not your day, is it?
GREG	Oh?
PHILIP	Sorry. I have an aunt who's eligible. Has been eligible for years, so she might not be quite what you're looking for. Though if you're desperate, she might do you. Or there's my wife's cousin Natalie who seems to want cheering up -
GREG	No. It's only your daughter I'm really interested in.
PHILIP	Then I'm afraid you're right out of luck -
GREG	Why?
	(GINNY enters from D.S. door with four glasses - moves to L.C.)
GINNY	Hallo.
PHILIP	Oh, hallo, Ginny.
GREG	Hallo.
GINNY	(nervously) Well. You're both looking solemn.
PHILIP	No, no - (Turns U.S., then right round to look at GREG.)
GREG	Yes.
	(Pause.)

GINNY   Anything wrong?

GREG   No. No.

(GINNY sets two glasses on the table.)

Your father was just telling me something.

(GINNY stops at U.S. of table. PHILIP turns to look at GREG in amazement. Pause.)

GINNY   Was he?

GREG   He seems to want me to marry his aunt now –

PHILIP   Who?

GREG   Your aunt –

PHILIP   Who did you say told you that?

GREG   You did.

GINNY   Your aunt!   (Laughs gaily.)

(PHILIP shushes GINNY, then turns to GREG.)

PHILIP   What did you call me?

GINNY   (puts two remaining glasses on table)   Oh dear, how stupid of me. I bet you two haven't even been introduced properly, have you?

GREG   ) Of course, we have!
PHILIP) Of course, we have! Don't be so silly.

GINNY   Daddy, this is Gregory, the one I've told you so much about. Gregory, meet my father.

(Slight pause. Then PHILIP moves to GREG and shakes him by the hand.)

PHILIP   (genially)   How do you do, old boy, how do you do. (Turns to GINNY.)   Yes!

CURTAIN

Scene 2

The same. An hour or so later.

The four are seated round the table. They have just finished lunch. GINNY is smoking a cigarette; GREG is smoking a cigar.

SHEILA   Has everybody had enough?

GINNY   Thank you.

GREG   Marvellous.

PHILIP   More than enough!   (Starts to light his cigar.)

SHEILA   Good.   (She rises.)   Just a moment. I'll fetch us some coffee.

GREG   Can I help?

SHEILA   No, no, thank you. It's all quite ready. I've only to bring it out.   (She goes through D.S. door.)

GREG   Your mother can certainly cook a meal, I'll say that.

GINNY   Yes. Can't she?

PHILIP   She's a fine wife and mother.

GREG   Have you always lived in the country?

PHILIP   Oh, yes. Ever since Ginny was – so high.

GINNY   Yes.

PHILIP   You could say this garden has watched her grow up, couldn't you, Ginny?

GINNY   Yes.

PHILIP   Sometimes, you know, in the long summer evenings, her mother and I sit here, she with her cigar – I mean me with my cigar and she with her knitting – and between us we can still picture her as she was then, just as if it were today – scampering over that rockery.

GREG   Really?

PHILIP   Funny little thing she was then. Very plump little girl, she was.

GREG   Was she?

PHILIP   Oh yes. In fact one could almost say fat. Certainly overweight.

GINNY   Daddy –

PHILIP   Her mother and I were quite worried about it. Almost <u>circular</u>, she was –

GREG   I'd never have guessed that –

GINNY   Daddy's exaggerating, as usual.

PHILIP   (warming to the subject)   Remember the nickname we used to have for you, Ginny? Do you remember?

GINNY   No, Daddy, it's all forgotten.

GREG   What was that?

GINNY   Nothing, nothing.

GREG   What was it?

PHILIP   (convulsed with laughter)   Jumbo!

GREG   Jumbo?

PHILIP   Jumbo Ginny – very funny I thought.

GREG   Jumbo Ginny, it's rather good.

    (They laugh.   GINNY glowers.)

GINNY   How very childish.

PHILIP   Yes, but you were only a child then, weren't you?

GINNY   But I'm not now.

PHILIP   Flat feet she had, too. I can remember them very clearly. Big flat feet – used to thunder round the place like a tram –

GINNY   I did not.

PHILIP   You were too young to remember.

GREG   She's changed a lot anyway.

PHILIP   Oh yes, yes. She has. I always think it's very lucky that you never know the person you're in love with when they're children. I mean, I wonder if you'd have felt the same about Ginny, Greg, if you'd known her with strawberry jam round her face, or when she had that skin trouble, or before her teeth were straightened –

GINNY   Daddy, please shut up. Greg isn't in the least interested.

PHILIP   I've got some photos somewhere, Greg. I'll show them to you before you go. Think you'll find them amusing.

    (SHEILA enters through D.S. door carrying a tray of coffee things.)

SHEILA   Here we are.   (Sets tray down on stool D.R.)   Now. Black or white for everyone? Ginny?

GINNY   Black, please.   (Rises and moves to SHEILA.)

SHEILA   (pouring coffee)   I'm so glad we decided to come outside. It's so stuffy indoors.   (Hands coffee to GINNY, who wanders U.S.)   There you are. Greg?

GREG   White, thank you. Yes, I was just saying, this is a great place to grow up.

SHEILA   Yes, I suppose it is.

GREG   I mean the air, to start with –

SHEILA   Oh, yes. And the soil.   (Hands coffee to GREG.)

GREG   Soil?

SHEILA   It's very rich just around here.

GREG   I was thinking, more, that there was somewhere to play.

SHEILA   Play? Are we talking about flowers or children?

PHILIP   Black.

GINNY   Flowers.

SHEILA   Black flowers? Oh yes, flowers, I thought we were.

GREG   Were we?

SHEILA   I beg your pardon?

GREG   I thought we were talking about children.

SHEILA   Really? How did we get on to that subject?

PHILIP   The soil round here is renowned for bulb growing.

SHEILA   Yes, that's very true. Famous for it.

GREG   Is it?

PHILIP   Definitely.

         (GINNY sits in canvas chair. GREG puts milk in his coffee.)

SHEILA   (putting cup on table)   There you are.

PHILIP   Thank you, darling.

SHEILA   (moving back to pour last cup of coffee)   You know, I just can't get over this weather.

GINNY   Yes. It's a pity really, that Greg and I will have to be leaving soon.

SHEILA   Oh, will you?

GREG   Will we?

PHILIP   What a shame.   (Rises eagerly and moves below table.)

SHEILA   Don't go on our account, will you? We've nothing planned for the rest of to-day, have we, Philip?

         (PHILIP returns dejectedly to sit at table. Pause.)

PHILIP   Hang on, hang on – aren't we supposed to be going out?

SHEILA   No. Where?

PHILIP   I forgot to tell you. The Coopers telephoned. They want us to go round there for tea.

SHEILA   When?

PHILIP   As soon after lunch as we can make it. I forgot to tell you.

          (GREG sits in cane armchair.)

SHEILA   I thought the Coopers were in Italy.

PHILIP   Back yesterday.

SHEILA   They only went on Wednesday.

PHILIP   Currency restrictions.

          (SHEILA moves U.S. of table.)

          They'd run out of lire by Thursday night.

SHEILA   Oh, what bad luck.

PHILIP   Wasn't it? I thought we'd better go over and console them.   (To GREG and GINNY.)   Our friends the Coopers.

SHEILA   (sitting at table)   They had been looking forward to it, too.   (To GREG and GINNY.)   It does look as if we'll have to pop over and see them. I am sorry about this.

GREG   That's all right.

SHEILA   I hate to think that we're driving you away.

GINNY   No, we do have to go.

GREG   (to her)   Why?

GINNY   (to him)   We have to.

SHEILA   What?

GREG   We have to.

SHEILA   If you're quite sure –

GREG   (to GINNY)   Why?

GINNY   Ssssh!

SHEILA   (to GINNY)   Do you live in London?

PHILIP   Greg?

GREG   Yes, I've got a couple of – rooms.

SHEILA   That's nice.

GREG   Well, one room with a washstand down the middle, really.

SHEILA   How interesting.   And how about - ?   (Turning to
         GINNY.)

GINNY   (interrupting swiftly)   I've got the same flat, of
         course.

SHEILA   Have you?

GINNY   Yes.

SHEILA   Yes, of course. Is it nice?

GINNY   Oh, of course, you've never been to see me, have you?

SHEILA   No, of course we haven't -

PHILIP   Neither of us has.

GINNY   No. Well, you must both come some time. They'd
         like it, wouldn't they, Greg?

GREG   Yes.

SHEILA   Thank you.

GREG   Besides, you ought to see what sort of conditions
         she's living in.

SHEILA   I wouldn't want to intrude.

GINNY   You're very welcome.

SHEILA   I'm not often in London, really. Of course, Philip
         goes, but I find the traffic and clatter gets me down
         so much. I'm a real country bumpkin, I'm afraid.

GINNY   I think you get used to it.

SHEILA   Depends where you were brought up, I suppose.

GINNY   Yes.

SHEILA   Were you born in London or in the country?

         (GINNY chokes on her coffee. She rises, coughing,
         puts her cup down and moves towards U.S. door.
         GREG rises and follows her.)

PHILIP   Steady, steady -

SHEILA   Are you all right?   (She rises.)

         (PHILIP rises and moves towards D.S. door.)

GREG   Ginny -

GINNY   (gasping)   Just - the coffee - could I possibly get
         - a glass of water?

SHEILA   Yes, of course. I'll fetch one -

GINNY   No, no - it's all right. I'll manage.

(GINNY goes into the house through U.S. door.
PHILIP stands at the D.S. door shouting and
gesticulating.)

SHEILA   (looking after her)   I ought to go with her.

PHILIP   She'll be all right.

SHEILA   Poor thing. I know what it's like.

GREG   It's all right, I know what's worrying her – her
            trouble.

SHEILA   Yes, you pour it down your windpipe –

GREG   And you know the cause –

SHEILA   It's a valve that doesn't open properly.

            (PHILIP sits at table.)

            It sticks – like that.   (She indicates.)

GREG   Really? I didn't know that.

SHEILA   (moving to table, picking up her coffee cup)   Neither
            did I, before.   (Moves towards stool.)   More
            coffee, anyone?

GREG   No, thanks.

SHEILA   Poor girl, I hope she's all right.

PHILIP)
GREG   )   She'll be all right.

SHEILA   I must say she's very sweet. I've quite taken to her,
            Philip.

            (GREG starts laughing. PHILIP stares at him, then
            joins in.)

            What does that mean?

GREG   I hope you have.

PHILIP   Rather!   (He and GREG are again convulsed with
            laughter.)

SHEILA   (laughing uncertainly)   Yes.   (Sits in canvas
            chair.)

GREG   Do you miss her?

SHEILA   Mmmm?

GREG   I mean – would you rather she lived nearer, rather
            than in town?

SHEILA   That's up to her, surely?

GREG   You don't look the worrying sort, anyway.

PHILIP   Oh, no. We don't let it worry us.

SHEILA   What?

PHILIP   The thought of people living in town. We don't let it worry us, do we?

SHEILA   I can't say we do.

GREG   That's a very healthy attitude.   (Moves to sit in cane armchair.)   It doesn't do any good at all, does it? Nine times out of ten if parents fuss too much they simply alienate their children.

SHEILA   You think so?

GREG   It's a fact.

PHILIP   Very true.

SHEILA   Yes.   (Pause.)   Do you play bridge?

GREG   Not at all.

SHEILA   What a pity. Seeing as there are four of us –

          (Pause.)

PHILIP   Talking of trains. (He rises.)   I think there's a good one back to town   (Looks at watch.)   in about an hour.   (Sits down again.)

GREG   Oh?

PHILIP   Yes. If you both stroll quietly down to the station, take your time about it, enjoy the walk, take advantage of the sunshine, get a good breath of air, look round the village, stretch your legs – you really ought to start getting ready.

GREG   Oh, right.

SHEILA   It's only a five minute walk.

PHILIP   No, but they have to allow a bit longer, especially if they want to take their time.

GREG   Yes, in that case –   (Swallows coffee, puts cup down and rises. Moves R.C.)

SHEILA   (stopping him)   There's really no hurry.

GREG   I think we'd better.   (Makes for his bag on terrace.)

SHEILA   As you wish. Anyway, you've got a lovely day for it.

GREG   I hope I'll see you again before long?

PHILIP   Surely. Surely.

SHEILA   I do hope so.

GREG   In case I don't and you should worry about her at all,
          I'll be keeping an eye on her. Keep her out of trouble.

SHEILA   Trouble? Has there been any trouble?

GREG   Yes, in a way.

SHEILA   What was that?

GREG   She hasn't told you?

SHEILA   Not a word.

GREG   Oh. Then I don't know that I should say anything –

PHILIP   No, I don't know that I should.

SHEILA   (rising and moving on to terrace)   Oh, don't be so
          mean. I want to know. What was it?   (Confidentially.
          Something – unpleasant?   (Sits at R. of table.)

          (PHILIP is still sitting at L. of table and GREG is
          standing between them U.S. of table.)

GREG   Well, yes.

SHEILA   (agog)   What?

GREG   Well – peculiar company – that sort of thing.

SHEILA   Peculiar company?

GREG   Yes.

SHEILA   Well? Go on, go on. You can't stop there.

GREG   I don't know that she'd want me to tell you.

SHEILA   I'm very broad-minded. You don't have to worry.

GREG   She hasn't confided in me to any great extent. It
          appears though, that she got herself mixed up with an
          older man.

SHEILA   Did she?

GREG   Not that there's anything wrong in that, I suppose.
          But he seems to have played her around a bit.

SHEILA   Played her around?

GREG   He was married and so on. Anyway, she had the
          sense to get out.

SHEILA   Quite right too.

PHILIP   I – er –

SHEILA   Yes, dear?

PHILIP   Nothing.

SHEILA   Poor girl. Did you hear that, Philip? Poor girl.

PHILIP   Yes. I was just going to say that there were probably two sides.

SHEILA   Nothing but selfishness on his, I should think.

PHILIP   I don't know.

SHEILA   I do.

PHILIP   How do you know?

SHEILA   It's obvious. I mean, what could he offer her?

PHILIP   It depends on the sort of man he was.

SHEILA   I can't see that that makes an awful lot of difference.

PHILIP   If he was, say, for instance, a rather remarkable man.

SHEILA   If he was all that remarkable he wouldn't be carrying on behind his wife's back, would he?

PHILIP   Unless he had a singularly unremarkable wife.

SHEILA   Probably his fault if she was. Presumably he was quite happy with her when he married her.

PHILIP   Perhaps she proved a bit of a disappointment, though. Pretended to be something she wasn't and then turned out to be quite different.

SHEILA   He probably did the same to her.

PHILIP   That's possible.

SHEILA   She didn't sneak off and carry on behind his back, though, did she?

PHILIP   How do I know she didn't? You tell me. I don't know.

SHEILA   I don't know. I'm just supposing, like you are.

PHILIP   Who says I'm supposing?

SHEILA   Aren't you?

PHILIP   Yes. Yes. I am – but – well, there's two sides to everything, that's all I'm saying. I think I've proved my point.

SHEILA   Rubbish. You haven't proved anything. It's painfully clear what sort of man he was.

PHILIP   Not at all.

SHEILA   Some tired businessman playing around with a young
           girl because he was bored.

PHILIP   I bet he was bored.

SHEILA   And throwing her away like an old boot when he'd
           finished with her.

PHILIP   Has it ever struck you that she might have seduced
           him?

SHEILA   Oh, come.

GREG   Doesn't sound likely.

SHEILA   Of course it doesn't.

PHILIP   You don't know what happened.

SHEILA   Do you?

PHILIP   No. Yes. No.   (Rises – moves D.R.)   But if I
           did – know what happened, I know what would have
           happened. Mincing round the office in a skirt that
           was far too tight and a damn sight shorter than anyone
           else was wearing – sort of coy and forward at the same
           time – well, you can tell. You can tell when a girl's
           looking for something like she was. Well – she got it.
           I expect.   (Crosses on to terrace to go off through
           U.S. door, spluttering.)   Excuse me. I must get a
           glass of water – excuse me.

SHEILA   (rising and looking after him)   Well, really! I've
           never heard anything quite so rude in my life. I'm so
           sorry. I don't know what you must be thinking.

GREG   I think it's more worrying than anything.

SHEILA   I haven't seen him like that for ages. Good heavens,
           he was almost involved.

GREG   I hope you don't mind my saying this – after all, he is
           your husband – but he does appear to me to be quite
           definitely a bit unhinged.

SHEILA   Have you noticed that?

GREG   It's difficult not to.

SHEILA   You're quite right. I was afraid it was just me.
           Everyone else I know seems to regard him as
           perfectly normal.

GREG   Hardly.

SHEILA   Do you think he's a psychopath?

GREG   Possibly.

SHEILA   I did whisper something to that effect to the doctor
         when he was last here.

GREG   What did he say?

SHEILA   I don't think he quite heard.   He's rather deaf.

GREG   Ah.   There's this business over Ginny just now. Let's
         face it, from the way he was talking, he didn't seem to
         give a damn about her, did he? I mean, the way I look
         at it, just because of some misconduct in the past, he's
         trying his best to disclaim her.   But when you boil it
         down, she's just as much his daughter as yours — if
         not more so.   (Sits on bench on terrace.)

SHEILA   Mine?

GREG   That's the way I look at it.

SHEILA   She's not my daughter.

GREG   I mean — to shrug off what happened to her, even to
         defend the man.

SHEILA   She's not my daughter.

GREG   That's bordering on irresponsibility of the worst sort.

SHEILA   She's not my daughter.

GREG   Mmm?

SHEILA   I don't know where you got that idea from.

         (GREG sighs.   He looks at her resignedly.)

         You're joking, aren't you?

         (GREG shakes his head.)

         You must be. My daughter. You haven't thought that,
         have you? No, you can't have done.

         (GREG sinks his head in his hands.)

         (Laughing nervously.)   You're pulling my leg.

GREG   (looks up)   She's not your daughter?

SHEILA   Certainly not.

GREG   (putting cigar out in ashtray on bench)   You still
         see it that way, do you?

SHEILA   No relation of mine at all.

GREG   (rising and moving to her)   You don't know how sorry
         I am to hear you talk like this.

SHEILA So am I. Hulking great girl.

GREG It's about time you tried to come to terms with this, isn't it?

SHEILA I'm afraid I don't follow you.

GREG Why, why, why turn your back on it? Ignore something that happened over twenty years ago? What's the point?

SHEILA I'm afraid I'm very lost now.

GREG We talk about your husband's attitude but yours is twice as dangerous.

SHEILA What?

GREG (getting excited) What do you think it's like for a girl to grow up in this sort of atmosphere? No wonder she came near to ruining her life. With a father who's a moral schizophrenic and a mother who refuses to admit her existence at all.

SHEILA Oh, poor girl.

GREG Yes, poor girl.

SHEILA I didn't know. How terrible.

GREG You do see that, then?

SHEILA Oh yes. I do. No wonder.

GREG Yes.

SHEILA It is irresponsible, isn't it? People of that sort really shouldn't have children at all, should they?

GREG They haven't faced up to it, that's what it is.

SHEILA Indeed they haven't –

GREG You get what I'm driving at?

SHEILA Oh yes, I do. I do. I do.

GREG Fine.

SHEILA I'm not her mother though. (Moving off terrace.) Please let's get that straight.

 (Pause.)

GREG (deep breath) This is the first and last time I try and do things the proper way. Let me tell you that. It just so happened that I was fond enough of Ginny to spend nineteen and six cheap day return, valid for one day only, to come and see her parents. Big gesture by me that was. Nineteen and six – ye gods – and what do I get? A couple of people who are so

wrapped up in themselves they couldn't care less
whether I came or not.   (Moving away from her.)
No wonder she tried to stop me coming down. If I had
parents like you two I think I'd volunteer for an
orphanage.

SHEILA You know, you really are completely mad.

GREG   I think I must be. Nineteen and six – that's nearly a
quid, do you realise that?

SHEILA Nobody asked you to come.

GREG   True.

SHEILA Either of you, as far as I know. You both crashed in
here uninvited –

GREG   Crashed in? I'm off –   (Crosses quickly towards
his bag U. R.)

SHEILA And you got a free meal. I don't know what you're
complaining about.

GREG   A free meal?   (Comes back.)   Oh, I am sorry.
Haven't I paid you for that? I did mean to. Just a
moment, I'll settle up with you.

SHEILA Oh don't be so silly.

GREG   I insist.   (Gets his bag and puts it on stool R. C.)
I'll settle for both of us whilst I'm about it.

SHEILA What on earth are you doing?

GREG   (rummaging)   Looking for my wallet.

SHEILA Oh, really.

GREG   (continuing search)   How much do I owe you? Would
ten bob cover us both? Sorry I can't afford any more.

SHEILA I don't know what's got into you.

GREG   (producing sponge bag and slippers)   Here, hold
these, will you?

SHEILA (taking them automatically)   All I said was, if you
really begrudge the fare that much, why did you come?

GREG   It's here somewhere.

SHEILA Oh send a cheque if you really want to.

GREG   No. Here we are.   (Produces wallet.)   Now, ten
bob, was it? Um –   (Looks inside and sees it is
empty. Dives into trouser pocket.)   I'll have to make
it seven and six.

SHEILA   I refuse to take it.

GREG   (slamming it on table)   There. Seven and six. I'll
          post you the extra half-crown. Don't bother to send
          a receipt.   (Puts sponge bag, jacket and raincoat
          in grip.)

SHEILA   Thank you.

GREG   (briskly)   That's the lot, isn't it? I think so.
          Right. I'll just find Ginny and then we'll be off.
          (He moves to house.)

SHEILA   I - What about your slippers?

GREG   They're not mine. Keep them.

SHEILA   Whose are they?

GREG   Better ask her that.

SHEILA   They're not hers?

GREG   They were in her flat.

SHEILA   What am I supposed to do with them?

GREG   I don't know. Give them to your husband or something.

SHEILA   Thank you, but he's already got a pair just -

GREG   I'm off then.   (Goes into house through U.S. door.)

SHEILA   Got a - just like -   (Shrieks.)   Wait!

GREG   (stops, leaves his bag inside and comes back.)
          What?

SHEILA   (recovering)   I was just looking at these slippers -

GREG   What about them?

SHEILA   Nothing. It's just that they're about my husband's
          size. I think he might be very glad of them.

GREG   Good. Yes. Yes, I'm sure he would - you keep
          them.

          (PHILIP and GINNY enter. GINNY carries GREG's
          bag and their coats.)

PHILIP   She's recovered at last.

GINNY   Sorry I couldn't stop coughing.

SHEILA   Better now?

GINNY   Thank you.

SHEILA   It must have been very awkward for you.   (She
          hides slippers in urn.)   I should sit down and

enjoy the sunshine while you can, before you go.
(Picking up tray.)   I'll just go into the kitchen. If
I can just get a little clearer then we can all have a
chat.

PHILIP   Grand.

(SHEILA goes out through U.S. door. GINNY and
PHILIP exchange a quick glance. GINNY moves to
GREG.)

GINNY   Come on, Greg – time we were going.

GREG   There's no rush.

PHILIP   Hold on, Ginny, old girl –

GINNY   We're going.

PHILIP   Greg and I haven't had a chance for a final chat.

GINNY   And you're not going to.

PHILIP   That's no way to speak to your father, Ginny.

GINNY   Oh – you great – goodbye. Come on, Greg.   (She
makes to leave.)

PHILIP   Now, now, now.   With your permission, Ginny. As
far as I understand it, you two want to get married,
is that it?

GREG   Ah, the penny's dropped.

GINNY   Thank you. Nice of you to realise that.

PHILIP   Greg – there is a special favour I'd like to ask of you
before you go.

GINNY   No.

PHILIP   Now don't jump down my throat, Ginny, before I've
finished.

GREG   Just a second, darling.

PHILIP   (humbly)   Thank you, Greg. Sit down a moment.

GREG   Thanks.   (He does so.)

PHILIP   This – well, it's in the nature of a personal favour,
Greg. You're entitled to say no, of course, if you
feel it's too much of an imposition. It's entirely up to
you, as I say. The fact is, I had planned in a few
weeks a little surprise for Ginny. You see, I always
promised her mother that, before Ginny was – taken
from us, as it were, I'd give her one really big
present that she'd remember us by all her life.

GINNY   Present?

GREG   What's that?

PHILIP   In just over a month I'm going on a long business trip
          to the Continent. It's a sort of grand tour of
          inspection of all our foreign branches. Take about
          six weeks - France, Germany, Italy, Spain,
          Switzerland, Holland, Denmark and Sweden.

GINNY   Good. Have a nice time, won't you?

PHILIP   (putting an arm round her)   I'd like to take you with
          me.

GINNY   You what?

PHILIP   I'd like you to come with me.

GINNY   What?

PHILIP   What do you say, Greg?

GREG   Um -

GINNY   No. No!

GREG   Six weeks?

PHILIP   Not for long, is it?

GREG   A lot can happen in six weeks.

GINNY   You're telling me.   (Backing away from PHILIP.)

PHILIP   Yes, I know it's a big thing to ask of you, Greg.
          You've every right to say no. But if you do both agree
          not only will you have done something for Ginny, but
          you'll have the satisfaction of knowing you've made a
          father very happy.

GREG   Well.

PHILIP   Is it too much to ask?   (Smiling.)   Hmmm?

GREG   Yes. See what you mean.   (He ponders for a moment.)
          O.K.

GINNY   Greg!

PHILIP   (deeply moved - clasping GREG's shoulder)   Thank
          you. Are you sure? I could always cancel all the
          arrangements if you -

GREG   No - no - of course not.

GINNY   Greg, you can't agree to this. You're mad. Say you
          don't. Please!

GREG   I don't know - I mean - it's only your father -

GINNY   (to PHILIP)   If you think I'm going to let you get
away with this –

PHILIP   She would write. I'm sure she'd write, wouldn't you,
Ginny?

GINNY   Philip!

PHILIP   She's a good letter writer. Always writes to me when
she's away, don't you, Ginny?

GINNY   (freezing)   I –

PHILIP   Lovely letters. I've kept them all somewhere. I'll
let you read them sometime, Greg, when we're on our
own.

GINNY   You –

PHILIP   (briskly)   Now then, have you got all your things –
your coats, bag? Fine. You'd better be on your way
now – don't want to miss any more trains to-day, eh?

GREG   No – right. Yes.

GINNY   Philip –

PHILIP   Have a pleasant trip back.

GREG   We haven't said goodbye to your wife –

PHILIP   Oh, don't worry about that. I'll explain you had to
dash off.   (Hustling them towards the garden exit.)
See you again before long, I hope.

GREG   Yes, surely. Cheerio then.

PHILIP   Goodbye. Come on, cheer up, Ginny. It'll be a
wonderful holiday for you. I promise you, you'll enjoy
every minute of it. Bye!

(He is within an ace of having brought off his coup and
got rid of them both when SHEILA appears suddenly
from the garden and blocks the way out.)

SHEILA   Enjoy what?

PHILIP   Oh –   (Recovering.)   Just in time to see them off.

SHEILA   Really?

PHILIP   Yes. Goodbye then.

GREG   (somewhat confused – vaguely)   Goodbye.

SHEILA   What's Ginny supposed to enjoy?

GREG   A trip to the Continent.

SHEILA   Really. How lovely.

GREG   She doesn't seem to think so.

PHILIP   You're going to miss that train, you know –

SHEILA   No? You don't know what you're saying. I wish I'd
            had an opportunity like that when I was your age. I'd
            have gone like a shot.

PHILIP   Well, it's all settled anyway. Now, you'll both have
            to run for it – Bye –

SHEILA   How are you going? On your own?

GINNY   Um... no... no. It's not really finally decided.

GREG   They're both going.

PHILIP   In a manner of speaking.

SHEILA   Both?

GREG   Your husband thought he'd take Ginny along with him on
            his business trip.

PHILIP   I –   (Sits in canvas chair.)

SHEILA   Splendid.

PHILIP   Don't get the wrong – er – business, naturally –

SHEILA   Of course.

PHILIP   That's all it is.

SHEILA   Your idea, of course?

PHILIP   Yes – no – yes. In a manner of – cheerio then – I – er –

SHEILA   I see.

PHILIP   Yes.

            (Slight pause.)

            You're really going to have to – sprint – flat out – for
            that – train of yours –

GINNY   (nervously)   I don't think the idea will come to anything,
            anyway.

SHEILA   Why ever not?

GINNY   I'm not awfully keen, that's all.

SHEILA   I can't believe that. Where are you planning on going?

PHILIP   Nowhere special.

GREG   France, Germany, Italy, Spain, Switzerland, Holland,
            Denmark and Sweden.

SHEILA   And you're not keen?

GINNY   No.

SHEILA   What about you, Greg?

GREG   Well, it's up to Ginny really – if she wants to go.

SHEILA   She must.

GREG   It'll just mean our putting off getting married, that's all.

SHEILA   Why?

GREG   Well, if she's away –

SHEILA   When are you going?

PHILIP   A month – if at all.

SHEILA   That's plenty of time to get married. A month? That's ample time.

GREG   I don't know if that was quite the idea –

SHEILA   It seems obvious.   (Sweetly.)   Don't you agree, Philip?

PHILIP   Uh?

SHEILA   They get married as soon as possible.

PHILIP   Oh – yes, yes.

SHEILA   I should take advantage of the offer while he's in the mood, Greg. You won't get the chance of a honeymoon like this again in a hurry.

GREG   Oh.

PHILIP   Uh?

SHEILA   Will they – Daddy?

PHILIP   No.

GREG   Oh. That's a bit different. I thought we were supposed to wait until after she came back?

PHILIP   No, no, no. That was – just an idea I had. It occurred to me for some reason – I don't know why – that you might want to hold on for a bit.

SHEILA   Surely they don't?

GINNY   No. That was – Daddy's idea, not ours.

SHEILA   Oh – silly Daddy!

GINNY   Yes – silly Daddy!

(They laugh.   PHILIP over-genially.)

PHILIP   Silly old Daddy –

GREG   So we can go ahead then?

SHEILA   Philip?

PHILIP   What? Oh – yes, yes.

GINNY   Thank you – Daddy.   (She kisses him on the cheek.)

PHILIP   A pleasure.

GREG   Thanks.

(They shake hands.)

GINNY   (holding out her hand to SHEILA)   And thank you –
Mummy.

SHEILA   It was nothing darling – nothing. Do take good care
of yourself in the future, won't you?   (She smiles.)
Now you really are going to have to run for that train.

GINNY   Right.

SHEILA   Make sure you've got everything. Heaven knows when
we'll be seeing you again.

GREG   I'll – er – fix up about the wedding and so on – have
to come down again, I suppose. Get things sorted
out.

PHILIP   I don't think that will be necessary.

GREG   I'm not quite sure who pays for everything, that's all.

PHILIP   You do.

GREG   Oh.

GINNY   Goodbye, Daddy. Look after Mummy, won't you?

PHILIP   (rising)   As always. Don't forget Father's Day,
will you?

GREG   Goodbye.   (Shaking hands with SHEILA.)   Thanks
for everything.

SHEILA   It was a pleasure, Greg.

GREG   Nice to have met you.

GINNY   'Bye.

(GINNY and GREG go out U.L. SHEILA and PHILIP
look after them, waving.)

SHEILA   'Bye.

PHILIP   Goodbye.

(Pause.)

SHEILA   Quite wrong for each other of course. It'll be a disastrous marriage but great fun for them while it lasts.

PHILIP   I gather you've gathered the general gist of things.

SHEILA   Just a little gist – yes. I don't think there's any need to go to the Coopers now, is there?

PHILIP   No.   (He goes through gate.)

SHEILA   No.   (She starts putting plates and glasses on tray.) We'll have tea here, then. I'll tell you one thing, though. I'm awfully glad we haven't got a daughter, she'd be a terrible handful, wouldn't she?

PHILIP   Yes, you're right there. She would.   (He catches sight of slippers in urn. He picks them out of the urn and comes back through gate.)   Sheila! Sheila! What are these doing here?

SHEILA   I don't know, darling. You really ought to look after your things more carefully.

PHILIP   My things? They aren't mine.

SHEILA   Of course they're yours. I bought them for you.

PHILIP   No, they're not. They look a bit like them – same tartan, same sort of shape and texture.

SHEILA   Well then – they're yours.

PHILIP   No, they're not – the lining's different.

SHEILA   Uh?   (She takes slipper from him.)

PHILIP   Mine were red.

(SHEILA examines lining of slipper.)

SHEILA   So they were. Oh dear.

PHILIP   What?

SHEILA   I was just wondering how that poor boy was going to make out.

PHILIP   Never mind about that.   (He takes slipper from her.) Whose are these?

SHEILA   Wouldn't you like to know?   (She claps her hands delightedly and moves on to terrace, to go out through D.S. door, leaving PHILIP gazing at the slippers, dumbfounded.)

CURTAIN

ACT ONE, Scene 1

Single bed, unmade, U. C.
   Under it:
        Pair of slippers
        Pair of GREG's shoes

Screen U. R.
   Behind it:
        Bunch of flowers
        Two mugs and saucers
        Teapot with made tea
        Sugar basin
        Half-full bottle of milk
        One teaspoon

Chest of drawers R.
   Over it:
        Mirror
   On it:
        Vase of flowers
        Hand mirror
        Handbag
        Make up
        Comb
   In second drawer:
        Six chocolate boxes

Wastepaper basket below chest of drawers

Door to hall D. R.

Curtained alcove below door
   Behind curtain:
        GINNY's dress
           "   coat
        GREG's old holdall

Small table U. L. by bed
   On it:
        Telephone
        Telephone pad
        Vase of flowers
        Ashtray

Window U. C. (curtains partly drawn)

Easy chair D.R.
   On it:
         Doll

Folding coffee table D.L.
   On it:
         Cigarette packet
         Box of matches
         Ashtray
         Bowl of flowers

Two upright chairs L. and R. of table

Door to bathroom D.L.

Offstage R.:

Parcel containing box of chocolates (GREG)

Offstage L.:

Hairbrush (GINNY)
Four bunches of flowers (wet) (GREG)
Pair of trousers (GREG)
One clean shirt (GREG)
One crumpled shirt (GREG)
Tie (GREG)
Shaving kit (GREG)
Sponge bag (GREG)

ACT ONE, Scene 2 and rest of play

Chair D.L.

Stone bench D.L.
   On it:
         Ashtray

Three chairs on terrace, placed round table

Round table on terrace
   On it:
         Tablecloth
         Teapot with made tea, milk jug, sugar bowl with sugar
         Two teacups and saucers, marmalade pot and spoon
         Toast rack, toast

      Two small knives
      Two side plates
      Two napkins
      Sunday Times and Colour Supplement

Trolley U.S. on terrace
  On top shelf:
         Tray
  On lower shelf:
         Papers and magazines

Basket chair and cushion U.S. on terrace
Cane armchair and cushion D.R.C.
Canvas chair and cushion D.L.C.
Cane stool and cushion D.C.
  On it:
         Gardening box, containing:
           Secateurs,   gardening gloves
           Gardening book,   Trowel
           Some other garden implements
           String,   seed packets

On U.S. wall:
  Paint tin
  Garden spray
  Ashtray
  Plant in potholder, R. of gate

Offstage L.:

GREG's holdall, containing:
  Jacket, with wallet
  Sponge bag
  Slippers

Tray with decanter of sherry and four glasses

Tray for lunch, with:
  Tablecloth
  Four side plates
  Four large knives
  Four large forks
  Four dessert spoons
  Four small knives

Apron (GREG)
Apron (SHEILA)
Fruit bowl
Four table napkins
Four wine glasses
One unopened bottle of wine
One half-full bottle of wine
Two cigars
One cigarette (light for GINNY for Act II, Scene 2)
One box of matches
Coffee tray, with:
    Coffee pot with made coffee
    Milk jug
    Sugar basin
    Four cups and saucers
    Four teaspoons

Offstage R.:

Zinc tub and tools for crash effect, Act II, Scene 1.

PERSONAL

GINNY	Handbag (Act II)
	Comb
	Compact
	Lighter
	Cigarettes
GREG	Cuff links
	Handkerchief
	Lighter
	Three half-crowns
	Key ring
SHEILA	Dark glasses
	Wrist watch
PHILIP	Wrist watch